A Book Called *Stuart*

A TRUE LIFE STORY

STUART H. GOLLINGER

Dedication

I dedicate this book to the love of my life, my dear wife Jeri, who inspired me to be a better man than I ever was before we first met just by being herself: a sweet, kind, good-natured woman who trusted me completely to be by her side during all of our 27 years together.

Acknowledgment

I hereby acknowledge the love, patience, and sacrifices of my dear wife, Jeri, my parents, Gertrude and David, my sisters, Janet and Nancy, my Aunt Harriet and Uncle Bernie, my Aunt Irene and Uncle Brud, my daughter, Geri, and son, Brad, the Gollinger family members, and the special people noted herein who helped me to be successful.

Table of Contents

About the Author 6

Preface 8

My Family 1

My Father 12

My Mother 22

My Schools 27

My Work 52

My Personal Life 79

Epilogue 175

About the Author

Stuart H. Gollinger was most recently a Tax Attorney in the Legal Division of the Connecticut Department of Revenue Services, with a concentration in the corporation business tax, inheritance tax, and estate tax. Before joining the Department in 1991, he practiced law for several years in Westport, CT, with an emphasis in personal and corporate taxation, tax litigation, estate planning, and probate administration. Previously, he had been a Tax Attorney and Associate Tax Counsel with Olin Corporation in Stamford, CT.

Mr. Gollinger received a Bachelor of Arts Degree from Colby College, a Juris Doctor Degree from Suffolk University Law School, and an LL.M. in Taxation from the University of Miami School of Law. He is a member of the Connecticut and Florida Bars.

Page Blank Intentionally

Preface

Everyone deserves to have people in their lives who can help them and show them the way. To improve who we are, what we want to be, when we want it to happen, where we wish to do it, why we want it to happen, and how to go about getting there.

Many times, we think we can do everything by ourselves, but we must not forget we are not alone. We have family, friends, colleagues, and even mere acquaintances who drift into and out of our lives. All of them can make a difference in helping us to answer the questions of who, what, when, where, why, and how. I was very fortunate to have had not only a terrific family but also friends, colleagues, and acquaintances who made a difference in my life.

My father, David, and my mother, Gertrude, were undoubtedly the most important people in my life while I was growing up. But there were others in my family, especially Uncle Bernie and Aunt Harriet, who greatly helped me get to where I am today. And I was also very lucky to have crossed paths with three wonderful men in my life.

The first was my dear colleague and friend at the corporation in Stamford, CT, Kent A., who was likely the finest gentleman I ever knew. The second was the Tax Director at the Connecticut Department of Revenue Services, who hired me, Albert S., who was most definitely the saintliest man I ever knew. The third was my brother-in-law, Dennis D., who brought so much joy to me and all who knew him and displayed so much dignity while he was dying from pancreatic cancer. All these men were so special to me not because of what they accomplished in their work lives but rather because they unknowingly enlightened me with their virtues of patience, humility, kindness, compassion, forgiveness, understanding, and love.

So, I was positively influenced by these remarkable individuals and some others, to a lesser extent, who embodied those virtues and thereby provided excellent role models for me to follow. Everyone can find such people in their lives if they look for them and allow them to enter their lives to provide their inner beings with spiritual reinforcement of such virtues. We all have those virtues within us, but we often need others to help us discover them.

My Family

I was born on February 3, 1942, in Grace New Haven Hospital, now known as Yale New Haven Hospital, to Gertrude and David G. I have absolutely no recollection of the first year or two of my life, living in an apartment with them in West Haven, CT. In fact, I don't remember too much of my first 8 years other than what I'm telling you here. I lived in a second-floor flat of a three-family house at 1600 Chapel Street in New Haven, CT. Built in 1900, it was situated in between two apartment buildings on the street comprised of mostly older, multi-story houses in what can best be described as a lower-middle-class neighborhood. Before I was born, my father's mother, Gussie, had purchased the house as an investment for her two sons many years after she immigrated to this country and worked hard to make enough money to bring up my father, David, and his brother, Bernie.

Our house featured a good-sized porch outside of the first floor, with several steps leading up to the front door. On the second story outside of my bedroom was a window-enclosed porch that I remember being used only for storage, which in hindsight was a big waste of good space that I could well have used for myself if I had gotten a space heater during winters and a portable air conditioner during summers. Initially, there were only two bedrooms in that flat. Until I was age eight, I shared the second bedroom with my Sister Janet, who was four years younger than me. But then Nancy was born four years later than Janet.

Due to the limited space in our flat, Nancy's birth necessitated finding a third bedroom. The second-story landing with steps leading up to the third story had a larger-than-needed hallway, so part of that open space was enclosed to become my bedroom off the living room. I never knew the dimensions of my bedroom, but it was the size of a large walk-in closet by today's standards, located right next to the window-enclosed porch. It was just large enough to contain a twin-size bed, a small bureau, a small end table with a lamp on it, and a movable wardrobe closet for my hanging clothes. But there was not even room enough for a small desk, which, in retrospect, I could have used for my many years of studying while I attended school.

For at least the first several years of my life, Rose R. lived on the first floor. She was a kind, older lady who was the aunt of the famous cartoonist Al C., whom I remember meeting once. On the third floor was an unrelated family of five, with two brothers, a sister, and their parents. At that time, my Uncle Bernie, Aunt Harriet, and their then family of five, including Jon, Jill, and Cathy, were renting a flat in a house several blocks away. I never could understand why. But then they moved to the first floor of our house sometime in the mid to late 1950s, and Rose R. left to find a rental elsewhere. Due to the limited space in the flat downstairs, there was a bit of disruption some years later when my Aunt Harriet and Uncle Bernie welcomed the birth of their third daughter, named Millie. With no additional bedrooms, they had to rely on their ingenuity to make a small bedroom for her from a portion of a hallway leading from one of the other bedrooms, and it was even smaller than mine. But the six of them managed to fit into very close quarters for many years.

At that time, our neighborhood was truly a good, convenient, safe place to grow up in, with a pharmacy and beauty salon diagonally across the street. Down the street were a Finast Supermarket, a bakery, a tailor, and a local bar. Across that street was another larger pharmacy next to a small fruit and vegetable store. Our Doctor E. was located just a few houses away from there, and the Hebrew School and synagogue I attended were about four blocks away from where we lived. Edgewood Park was just a few short blocks up the street, and it had a nice duck pond that we used to walk by to get to an open field where we played football or the hills where we went snow sledding in winter. It also served as the site for the annual children's Easter Egg Hunt the day before Easter. Everything was within easy walking distance for us.

During the 1950s, I recall we received regular milk deliveries in glass bottles every few days. In addition, a small truck filled with various fresh fish came to our neighborhood, and we would always know it was near the sound of its distinct horn. The "Good Humor" ice cream truck also stopped by during the warm months, and an ice truck delivered big blocks of ice to people living in the adjacent apartment buildings who still used old ice boxes instead of the new refrigerators available. The ice truck driver was a very strong man who used a big ice tong to pick up a large block of ice and put it on a pad on his shoulder prior to delivery to the customer. During the summer, kids in the neighborhood would remove ice shards from the truck to quench their thirst and keep cool.

I think you should know that my Grandma Gussie was once married to my Grandpa Benjamin, but I never knew them as a couple. They were the first people in my young life who I learned were divorced. If you ever saw them together, you would know why they were mismatched. My Grandma Gussie was physically a big woman with a strong will and a loud voice. She came to this country from Poland before the turn of the 20th century on a steamship by herself at age 14 or 15. I could not even imagine how she managed to do that at such a young age. Her first known business venture was a toy store that she opened in the Washington Avenue area in New Haven, CT, when my father was about age 13. She later closed that store and founded what became a well-known furniture store located on State Street in New Haven called The Lincoln Furniture Company.

On the few times she visited us, I was usually the first one up in the early morning, and she would tell me all about her travels on Cunard's Queen Mary, which sailed primarily on the North Atlantic Ocean between New York and Southampton. I was maybe 8 at the time, and I was very impressed she traveled alone on such a big ship a few times. At breakfast, I remember Grandma Gussie would squeeze a lemon in a cup of hot water and tell me it would "clean her insides." She had lived for many years wintering in Miami Beach, FL, in an old, one-story bungalow not far from Collins Avenue. In summers, she lived in a small, somewhat run-down, unheated cottage located up a big hill in the Woodmont section of Milford, CT. She had a few friends nearby, and she seemed happy there. In March 1960, she deeded her title to our house to my father and uncle, and then she died a few years later at age 65 in Miami Beach while I was still away at college. In retrospect, she was the true matriarch of our family who came to this country as a young teenager and, with years of hard work, paved the way for her sons' success by creating and building a furniture business as a future nest egg for them, and purchasing the house our entire family of four adults and seven children lived in for so many years. I think Grandma Gussie never received enough credit, love, and respect from our family for what she accomplished. But I think it may have been simply because our parents never told any of us, including me, what she had done. For some reason, they kept it secret from us that Grandma Gussie had bought the furniture store as well as our house.

My Grandpa Benjamin, on the other hand, was a smallish, gentle, soft-spoken man who was born in Austria, emigrated to Vilnius in Lithuania, which was then part of Russia, to escape religious persecution, and also entered the US in the late 1890s. He was not really a businessman. But he had a craft as a furniture restorer who could fill in dents and scratches in all kinds of furniture, from dark mahogany to maple to light walnut, using a heated implement to melt resin sticks that matched most every furniture color. He was the one who first introduced me to fishing at a young age, taking me out in his rowboat to fish for porgies in Milford, CT, off Long

Island Sound. Just the two of us enjoying each other's company on a nice summer day.

And if I happened to work at the furniture store years later on an early Thursday afternoon during a school vacation, I was always sure where my grandfather was. He was off by himself at a movie matinee to see the latest western. When I came home from college and paid him a visit, he delighted in having me sample some of his homemade cherry brandy that he made from scratch. Gardening was also among his other hobbies, and he was always eager to show me his newest plants and flowers. I never remember my grandfather ever raising his voice in anger. He died in 1977 at age 88 in a nursing home not very far from where we lived.

My mother's youngest sister, Irene Arrick, succumbed to COVID at age 91 on July 20, 2020. She was the last member of the previous generation in our entire family and one of the most well-loved, for sure. She had been living in an independent living apartment in a rather chic assistant living facility in Miami, FL, called The Palace for the last five years of her life. Prior to that, she lived alone in a condominium in Pompano Beach, FL, for almost four years following the death of her husband, William "Brud" Arrick, on May 8, 2013, which was a little more than a year after my dear mother passed away. My

Aunt Irene was, without a doubt, one of the nicest, most pleasant, easy-going women I ever knew. She was always kind and good-natured and never raised her voice, yelled, or showed a temper towards anyone in all the years I knew her. She was also a very bright woman who constantly read books. In fact, I never knew her without having a book at hand to read. Jeri and I visited her at her condominium and apartment several times after we moved to Florida in 2011.

She was approximately thirteen years older than me. She told me she used to baby-sit for me, but I do have a vague recollection of being at her wedding to my uncle when I was about six or seven. I seem to remember Uncle Brud used to come to our house with a tennis racket under his arm when he was still dating Aunt Irene. Tennis was his favorite game. Years later, when I came home from vacation in college and law school, I enjoyed visiting my aunt and uncle in their cape home in the Westville section of New Haven and playing around with their two sons, Bruce and Stephen. I liked going there because it was always a calm and relatively quiet environment.

But I never really knew until just recently how and why one of the arms of Uncle Brud was disfigured because he never talked about it. But while he was still a Sophomore at the University of Virginia, the US Army called him to arms during World War II, and he soon thereafter found himself in a battle with the Germans in Aachen, Belgium, right on the German border in December 1944 during the early stages of the "Battle of the Bulge." There, he witnessed his entire infantry platoon being wiped out as he lay wounded in a foxhole. Somehow, he single-handedly managed to take out a German machine gun nest, and he survived. Many years later, even after his death, his sons found in his safe-deposit box the Silver Medal of Honor for valor in combat that had been awarded to him by President Harry S. Truman after the War in 1945.

Uncle Brud was as easy-going, soft-spoken, and pleasant a man as Aunt Irene was a woman. From the time I was still a young boy, I remember he had a shoe store in one of the first suburban shopping centers in Cheshire, CT, outside of New Haven. He had taken over the shoe business from his late father and operated the shoe store for many years. In 1967, many years before Cable Television and before the merger of the American Football League and the NFL, the NFL had a rather strange rule that NFL Championship games were "blacked out" in targeted areas played within the TV region of any NFL team. So, New Haven was one of the areas that "blacked out" for the New York Giants, but Cheshire, outside of New Haven, was not. So, my father and I went to watch the 1967 NFL Championship Game with my Uncle Brud on his 24-inch black and white television at his shoe store. The final score was Packers 21-Giants 17.

At the time, I was age 25 and the father of a baby daughter, Geri. My cousin Bruce, the older son of my Aunt Irene and Uncle Brud, was almost 10 years old, and his younger brother, Stephen, was 6 years old. Bruce grew up to graduate from the University of Florida and the University of Florida College of Law, and his younger brother, Stephen, attended Michigan State University and the University of New Haven, where I later taught an Income Tax course and a Business Law course for a few years while I worked for the corporation in Stamford, CT.

On January 21, 1984, Bruce married Susan Goldman, who also had become a lawyer. Bruce has had a long, successful career in his own private practice of law, and Stephen has worked for Del Monte Foods Inc. for many years. Bruce and Susan Arrick have three children: Adrienne, born in 1988; Ryan, born in 1992; and Trace, born in 1998. Adrienne married and had a son named Brayden, now 14.

For many years, our family had a dog named Lucky, which was a mixed breed of pointer, beagle, and even terrier. He was mostly black, with some white on his chest and some tawny feet. We must have gotten him before I was eight years old because I remember he used to lie under the crib where my baby sister Nancy slept.

Back in those days, dogs were not usually housebound. After eating in the morning, Lucky would leave the house with us when we were going to work and school, and he would walk all day long over the sidewalks and streets in and near our neighborhood. But every night, he would come home for dinner at the appropriate time. I remember a few times he came home with cuts and scrapes he had evidently incurred during the day in encounters with cats or dogs, and we'd take him to the veterinarian for treatment. He was a very obedient dog except when he saw the postman, and then he barked and even ran after him or his truck at times. He was with our family until he was 17. When I was away at college, my mother called to tell me that he was hit by a car crossing our street. By then, he had slowed down quite a bit and was not as fast as he used to be. We all loved Lucky. He was a good dog.

My Father

To this day, I still hear my father's words of wisdom in my head, saying things like "You have nothing without your health" or "Don't put off doing what you need to do today." What he said to me was especially compelling because he never had any formal education. But he learned by experiencing life, and he developed the best commonsense of anyone I ever knew. From the time I could walk, I remember my father and uncle owning The Lincoln Furniture store on State Street at the corner of Elm Street, right next to a Greek restaurant. Neither my father nor uncle ever mentioned that my Grandma Gussie originally purchased the furniture store for them after she had closed her toy store. It was a large five-story building nearly always filled with furniture.

On the basement floor, there were kitchen tables and chairs, kitchen appliances, and rolls and rolls of linoleum. The store office was on the rear of the first floor, which included living room sofas, chairs, tables, and lamps, with more on the second floor where the warehouse was located. The third floor included bedroom furniture, and the fourth floor included a work area where my grandfather fixed furniture. An interesting feature of the store in the front right window on the first floor was a large, revolving circular floor on which featured furniture was shown going slowly round and round.

My father worked very hard in his furniture store. He was in the store early every day, getting ready to map out the schedule of furniture deliveries with the delivery men. He was diligent and took charge of the day-to-day business of the store, including making regular purchases of furniture and usually taking care of sales to walk-in customers. My father was a born salesman, not because he knew so much about the furniture or its manufacturers, but because he could connect with people, from professionals to ordinary, everyday working-class men and women. He genuinely liked to talk to people and could start up conversations with anyone and everyone he met. And everyone liked him. Likewise, everyone liked my Uncle Bernie, who mostly handled the financing of furniture purchases and overall financial matters of the business. My Uncle Bernie was a very fine man with a more analytical brain than my father, but he also had a good sense of humor. And he meant an awful lot to me growing up.

During school holidays and on Saturdays when needed, I worked on the furniture truck with the delivery men carrying furniture. It seemed like most of the customers' houses were in multi-story houses like the one we lived in, and our deliveries always seemed to go to the top floors.

I remember trying to help lift a refrigerator, a big chest of drawers, or a long couch around the corner of a landing of steps leading to a second or third story that did not appear at all possible to navigate around. But somehow, the three of us always managed to do it. The driver and lead delivery man was originally from Ireland and still spoke with a slight brogue. His assistant was a young man, maybe around my age, who never went past high school. They were interesting for me to be with because they were so different from most of the people I knew. But I got along well with them. Occasionally, they would stop on the way to a delivery and get a quick beer in a local tavern. It was none of my business what they did so long as they did their work for my father. And they did it well.

Unfortunately, the furniture store had a major fire in June 1963, just a week or so after I had graduated from college. So, I ended up working there all summer, helping as much as possible to clean up the mess caused by the fire, which caused major damage to the furniture on the first floor and a great deal of smoke damage to the upper floors.

The store had a fire sale that took longer than expected into late August, requiring me to assist in selling furniture as well as delivering it. Looking back, I believe the various experiences I had working in the furniture store were important in helping to build my discipline and strength of character to overcome adversity in life.

About six years later, the furniture store was taken by eminent domain by the City of New Haven to build a parking lot, and the store was closed. My father and uncle looked around to find another way to make a living. They purchased The New Haven Motor Inn, a motel in New Haven just off the Wilbur Cross Parkway near the tunnel leading to Hamden. Neither of them knew anything about the motel business, but they learned on the go. The motel had many rooms spread out on several acres of land, which made it a somewhat difficult facility to maintain. At the time, the New York Football Giants were playing games in the Yale Bowl after Yankee Stadium was closed for a massive reconstruction. One of the teams they played in the pre-season was the New York Jets, whose players stayed at the motel prior to the game. It was the first time I had ever met professional football players in person. The Jets players were very talented at the time, comprised of many of the same players who later went on to win Super Bowl III on January 12, 1969.

My father and uncle loved to play golf and were both good at it, each with a lifetime seven handicap, something most weekend golfers, like me, will never see in our lifetimes. He and my uncle were long-time members of the Woodbridge Country Club in Woodbridge, CT. It's not that they had so much money to be able to afford membership in a private golf club, but rather how they chose to spend the money they made. Through the golf club, they both made long-time friends with doctors, lawyers, and other professionals who took an instant liking to them, and these members also provided a good source of customers for their furniture business. They were both well-respected by everyone who knew them as men of integrity and honor.

My father loved a beautiful car. And he always owned a great-looking car. When I was still a young boy in the early to mid-1950s, I remember he had an Oldsmobile 88 Convertible in sky blue that was the most stylish of any car I'd seen anywhere. Later, when I was in high school, he had maybe one the nicest cars I have ever seen to this day. It was a fire-engine red Lincoln Convertible with sleek, long fins in the back of the car on both sides. It was surely an eye-catcher. When I was 16 and had just gotten my driver's license, my father let me take the Lincoln out one night. The car was even bigger than I realized, and I tried to drive around the corner of a building in front of a parking lot in the back of the building. But I cut it a bit too close and put a dent in the driver's side door of the beautiful car. I thought my father would be rip-roaring mad at me and harshly discipline me, but he took it in stride and told me to just be more careful next time.

It seemed like a rather unusual reaction for my father, given he had physically punished me before on a few occasions while I was growing up. Most times, the anger he directed at me resulted from my mother telling him when he came home from a long day at work about what I had said or did that she thought was too mouthy, disrespectful, and deserving of punishment. The usual reaction for him was to take me to another room away from my mother and sisters, where he'd take off his belt and lash me with it until I could run away and seek refuge outside the house. I was more emotionally hurt by his abusive actions towards me than I was physically harmed.

There were times I wanted to run away from home rather than put up with my parents' abuse because I considered myself to be a good boy undeserving of such harsh punishment. But I always stayed and continued to hope for better days ahead. I often sought relief just by going downstairs to talk it out with my Aunt Harriet. She always listened and comforted me. She knew the emotional difficulty I had dealing with my parents at times, but she kept it between us. She helped get me through my teens in one piece. And I owed her an awful lot.

My father was the one who introduced me to politics in the Democratic Party in New Haven, which was then led by a powerful party boss who was personally a friend of his. In fact, one year, our family was invited to Christmas dinner at his house, which I shall always remember.

It was a feast of different seafood, turkey, ham, potatoes, fresh vegetables, wines to accompany all of it, plus delicious desserts.

I mention this to point out the fact that my father knew so many people in New Haven and its environs that he had friends from all different walks of life. He was actively engaged in politics for the local and State Democratic Party in Connecticut, both in fundraising and making calls to people he knew on behalf of Democrats running for Local, State, and National offices. Accordingly, he met them during their campaigns and introduced me to them when I worked at the local campaign headquarters. I know it must have given my father a sense of great pride and satisfaction that, despite growing up without much money and with no formal education, he could meet and help elect several notable State and local politicians.

It seemed like my father knew everyone no matter where we went: the Mayor of New Haven, the owner of the local movie theater in downtown New Haven, the guy shucking clams for us at the outdoor clam bar of a restaurant near the Savin Rock Amusement Park in West Haven, the long-time female owner of one of the oldest pizza restaurants on Wooster Street in New Haven, the guy taking tickets at Yale Bowl on Saturday afternoons, the salesman trying on my shoes at a local men's store, a downtown jeweler, the pharmacist in the drug store across the street from the furniture store and, of course, the owner of the good Greek restaurant located next door to the furniture store, where my father had lunch every day. It had the best rice pudding I've ever had, and its pea soup was terrific, too. My father's acquaintances were everywhere in the local area. Everyone knew his name, even if he didn't always remember theirs, which was mostly the case.

Following several years of ownership of the motel, my father and uncle sold their interests and went their separate ways. My uncle ventured into becoming a local real estate salesman, and my father was hired by an acquaintance from the country club who owned a local Cadillac dealership. My father knew even less about cars than furniture, but he knew Cadillac was a quality automobile. In his first year at the dealership, he sold more new cars than any other salesman there. And so, he won a trip for my mother and him to Bermuda. How did he do it? With his great personality…by selling himself more than selling the quality of Cadillacs. Customers loved to come in and ask for Dave because he was so well-liked. He had a gift of gab by just being himself, with absolutely no pretenses.

From the time I was a young boy, I remember my father smoked "Camel" cigarettes. Maybe up to three packs a day? He also liked to eat. That's why we always had my mother's good, home-cooked meals every night. But he also treated us often to go out to dinner on weekend nights at local restaurants. We all liked pizza from our favorite restaurant on Wooster Street, which still features photos on the walls of famous celebrities who ate pizza there, including a man who became President of the United States sitting next to his wife, who should have been elected President. My father also took us out to dinner at good Italian, Chinese, and American restaurants all over the New Haven area. And there were many, even for a city of its size. It's no wonder my father, Sister Janet, and I were all overweight because we liked to eat, and we certainly did eat well.

When my father reached age 65, he had a heart attack and spent several days in the hospital recuperating. He was indeed fortunate that he survived because other overweight, heavy cigarette smokers do not often get another chance at life, and they die from the first heart attack. I remember my father telling me afterward that the doctor read him the riot act, warning him that he had to stop smoking and lose weight; otherwise, he would not be around long. What happened afterward was something none of us ever thought possible. With the kind of personal self-control we had never seen before, my father never touched another pack of cigarettes, and he also changed his eating habits and lost a lot of weight. I would have guessed my father, at his heaviest, may have tipped the scales at nearly 250 pounds. But later in life, he may have been just under 200 pounds, and he looked very different.

My Mother

My Mother, Gertrude, was the oldest of three sisters, Norma (Noni) and Irene, and she also had a brother, Nathan, who always lived somewhere else, so we only met him on a few occasions. They were the children of Sarah and Samuel L., the grandfather I never knew. He was a window glazier who worked on the construction of the Empire State Building in New York City, and his name is on a plaque on its entrance wall as one of the featured tradesmen who helped to construct the building in 1930-1931. Unfortunately, he died in a work-related accident not long thereafter, when my mother was still a young teenager.

Neither my mother nor grandmother ever wished to talk about what happened. So, I never pressed them. But I was named after him. The photos I've seen of him reveal a nice-looking bald man with a big smile who died way too early in his life. Looking back, I never asked or was ever informed whether my grandmother ever received any compensation due to the tragic death of my grandfather.

My mother, Gertrude, was always an attractive, petite, five-foot-high woman with light brown hair and in good shape. She was a stay-at-home housewife who spent her time cooking and cleaning in our flat. And when she wasn't doing that, she was either hanging clothes on a line off the outside porch next to the kitchen on the second floor, or she was reading a book. She always liked to read. We didn't have a clothes dryer because there wasn't room for it in our small kitchen. So, a clothesline had to be attached off the little porch on the second story to a tall pole in the backyard.

One day, when I was a little boy, I remember a man who seemed as wide as he was tall came into the backyard with a long pole, the size of a regular telephone pole, on his right shoulder. He dug a hole in the ground and somehow managed to put the pole into the hole he had dug, which was filled with concrete to keep the pole from ever falling. At the time, there was nothing in the backyard but a few small lilac trees, the tall pole, and two trees adjacent to the apartment building next to our house. Several years later, a three-car garage was built there, where a backboard and basketball rim were attached.

My mother was a very talented cook who learned much from her mother, Sarah, who had learned from her mother. But my mother's cooking well-surpassed the regular Jewish meals on Passover, Rosh Hashanah, and other holidays that my Grandma Sarah cooked for us. My mother loved pasta. It was her favorite dish. She learned much from an Italian cleaning lady who came to clean a few times, showing her how to make a delicious red tomato sauce with sweet sausage. It was one of my father's favorites, but so was my mother's Chicken Fricassee, lamb chops, roast beef, and kugel. In fact, there was nothing my mother could not cook. She could also bake well, but since my father, Sister Janet, and I were already overweight, we thought it best not to ask Mother to bake too much. Nevertheless, my mother could bake anything with the best of them, especially on Thanksgiving.

We were fortunate to have had a mother and wife who provided us with such a great diversity of meals, which included various chicken dishes, soups, steaks, and even good baked desserts. When she was not cleaning or reading, she made everything from scratch. She had learned from her mother how to make most of the soups and dishes she made for the Jewish holidays. When we visited my Grandma Sarah, I remember her standing by the stove, stirring a big pot of soup with a cigarette dangling from her mouth. Another thing I remember is that Grandma Sarah was wracked with terrible arthritis in her body, so much so that she required fusion surgery in an ankle to allow her to be able to stand on that foot. My mother would always remind us before we went there that Grandma Sarah was in constant pain.

By then, my Grandma Sarah had long since remarried a man also named David, who also had a surname beginning with "G." He, too, was bald, like my grandfather Samuel, but had a somewhat bigger frame, looking more like a Russian Bolshevik than what we would have expected to be our own step-grandfather. We only saw him when we visited Grandma Sarah, and he always sat in the same chair reading a Jewish newspaper, just nodding. In all the years we had Passover Seders at my grandma's house, I usually had too much wine because I was always so bored with the length of the Seder service. I don't ever remember any of us having many conversations with Dave G. because we didn't have anything in common with him except he was married to our grandma. Also, Dave G. never said much of anything, even during the Passover Seders, unless he read from the Seder Prayer Guide.

Sometime after the divorce of my Grandmother Gussie and Grandfather Benjamin, my grandfather married the widowed mother of one of my father's closest friends, Harry T. He and my father had been good friends for many years and were in the same card club playing gin or pinochle at least once every week at each other's home on a rotating basis. The card club included Kay K., Harry W., and Burt C. They played cards for years in the dining room of our flat, which was, for all intents and purposes, right next to my bedroom and the living room. It's a wonder I ever fell asleep listening to them talk, shuffle cards, and deal them out. I wish I had thought of earplugs back then. They would have saved me hours of sleepless nights tossing and turning.

While growing up, I did not have much interaction with my younger sister, Nancy, because of the eight-year age difference. When I went off to college at age 17, Nancy was still 9 years old. My Sister Janet, on the other hand, was close enough to my age to be a royal pain in the neck. She and I had many close encounters, and her instigations of some arguments over petty stuff caused me a lot of pain. Like when I punched her in her arm over some nasty things she said to me, I was severely punished by my father in the usual manner. But I think being a middle child also may have adversely affected her. She may have always felt she was unduly neglected. I remember that my mother constantly taught my sisters and me about proper etiquette, polite behavior, treating family members, friends, and acquaintances with good manners, acts of kindness, and, in general, sincere consideration of their well-being. And so, you could say my mother taught us how to become better adults.

My Schools

The Barnard Elementary School I attended was in an old brick building on Derby Avenue, a short three-block walk from our house on sidewalks on nearby Ellsworth Avenue leading down to Derby Avenue. Back in those days, children walked home for lunch and then went back to school in the early afternoon. I recall our classes had milk and Graham crackers about mid mornings, which I always looked forward to.

My friend, Arthur H., lived in an apartment building directly across the street from me, and my other friends who were one street over were Norman P., who lived in a house he and his mother shared with his aunt and uncle, and Stuie G. who also lived in an apartment house with his mother and older brother Dick. I remember being curious because I had never seen any of them with a father. But I later concluded I may have been the only one of us who had a father. I never asked any of them about it, but I should have.

All of them had birthdays well before mine in February. So, all of them were ready to go to kindergarten except me because I wasn't at least age five by the beginning of the school year, which began in September. I was very upset that all my friends were going to school and not me. So, I raised a ruckus with my parents, carrying on and on, questioning them why I couldn't go with my friends. No matter what they said, it wasn't good enough for me to understand. I guess they may have contacted someone at the Board of Education who relented and let me join my friends at school, although I was only four and one-half. I'm sure you realize that, years later, the age difference would be significant. But what did I know at that time?

I do not remember most of my teachers from my grammar school days in the early 1950s or even what I learned. But one day, when I was in the 3rd grade, it stuck out. It was a visiting day for parents one afternoon. And wouldn't you know it, I was caught speaking out of turn or being rambunctious in the morning, so when it was time for the parents to come into class. There I was, sitting on a stool facing a corner of the room, being singled out for being mischievous. I remember that I did not sit there for too long after my mother and other parents first entered the room. But I had to explain to my mother why I was there and, of course, it was not my fault.

When I was sick or didn't feel well enough to go to school, I'd stay in bed listening to the radio. We didn't have a television until I was age 8 in 1950 when I was able to see my first World Series between the Yankees and the Phillies. Up until then, I had to listen to a variety of different radio programs, from morning entertainment shows with Arthur Godfrey and others to suspenseful shows like "The Shadow," "Dragnet," and "Superman" at night. Ads on the radio were also interesting, listening to men and women talk about "Studebaker," "Ipana" toothpaste, "Carter's Little Liver Pills," "Arid Deodorant," "Chesterfield" cigarettes, and others. My favorite shows in the early days of television were "Amos 'n' Andy," "I Love Lucy," "The Texaco Star Theatre" with Milton Berle, "Ozzie and Harriet," "Your Show of Shows," with Sid Caesar Imogene Coca, Carl Reiner and Howard Morris, "The Ed Sullivan Show," "The Lone Ranger" and so many others.

My recollection of my first big problem at home was when I came home from school one day with a new bent ring that I had received from a classmate named Arthur B. in exchange for my Mickey Mouse watch. My mother was not very happy with my new ring that Arthur had apparently pulled out of a box of cereal, for which I had traded my watch that must have been purchased at a cost of at least $5 at the time. So, she marched me over to his house several blocks away, demanding that I retrieve my watch and give him back his ring. I never did find out how Arthur's ring got bent. Of course, that experience left me feeling ashamed of my failure to understand relative values. But I got over it when I realized that I had made a very dumb deal.

As a seven-year-old, my parents urged me to take piano lessons, given we had a big grand piano that filled a large portion of our living room. I learned to read sheet music and play many well-known songs on the piano. But looking back, I wasn't too good, and now I wish I had tried harder. A very large woman, Miss D., would visit me once a week to give me piano lessons. I'll always remember the first time she arrived in a rather small car for such a large woman, how it rose about two feet when she got out of the car. And then, when she got back in, the car would sink down just the opposite. My first thought as a little boy was, "That poor car, and how much damage she was doing to it?"

I continued playing the piano for several more years, but it was getting more and more difficult for me to keep up with it, given everything else I had to do going forward with all my regular and religious schooling. But sometimes I still miss playing the piano even today. I have even thought about purchasing a portable keyboard to play.

And I still might?

As a young Jewish boy, I was expected to go to Hebrew School two days a week after regular schooling, plus also go to Sunday school. The Hebrew School was in the same building where our synagogue was located, about a four-block walk from home. And I did that for seven long years. I used to commiserate with my Catholic friend, Dennis B., who lived a few houses away from me and had to go to Catechism classes at a Catholic church nearby as often as I went to Hebrew School. We both disliked having to go to our religious classes after school. My Hebrew School classes were relatively small, seating maybe 10 boys. I don't remember any girls in my classes. But I made some lifelong friends there, including one whose family made bagels in New Haven that are still sold in supermarkets all-across our country. One year, we encountered a teacher in Hebrew School who was a deft, left-handed chalk thrower with good aim when any of us were caught talking or not paying attention while he was speaking.

We all surely learned how to read Hebrew well, but I don't think we ever really learned to comprehend what we were reading without the aid of an English text on the page next to it. So, to this day, I can still pretty much read Hebrew, but I have no idea what it means. Saturday mornings, my friend Michael W. and I led the Sabbath services for the children in the congregation. I was the junior cantor, and Michael was the junior rabbi. We did so for at least a few years up until our own Bar Mitzvahs. Mine was held on February 12, 1955, and I remember being very excited. I must give special praise to our Rabbi K., a somewhat cuddly, five-foot man with a big heart, and Cantor L., with a terrific baritone voice that added much to the enjoyment of Sabbath services.

I thought they were both truly good at their jobs, and they helped me to succeed very well in learning the prayers and the songs for the Sabbath services and for my Bar Mitzvah. I was probably closer to Cantor L. because he had asked me to walk with his 6-year-old daughter to our grammar school the previous year. Around the time of my Bar Mitzvah, I started to become sort of interested in girls, particularly a pretty blond named Susan M., who I had seen at other Bar Mitzvahs. She and several other girls and my boy friends were invited to the afternoon Bar Mitzvah luncheon held in my honor at the local country club where my father played golf. I was all of five feet tall at that time, but some of the girls there were even much taller.

After my grammar school days were over, I attended T. Junior High School in New Haven, where schoolyard brawls between young girls during lunch recess were a common occurrence. You cannot believe what a catfight is like between two big girls pulling each other's hair, biting, and tearing their clothes to shreds? I thought they were even more frightening than the boys who just slugged it out. I learned very little in my one year there because it seemed like the classes taught more of the same things we had in grammar school, still doing multiplication and division. So, part-way through the school year, I complained to my father that I was not learning anything I didn't already know and needed a better education.

He knew an attorney with an office in downtown New Haven who was on the Board of Trustees at a local private school named Hopkins, whose origin went way back to 1660. I'm not kidding. The attorney recommended to my father that I take the Hopkins admissions test. And I did but didn't do very well based on my underwhelming grammar school education and probably my underachieving IQ at the time. Then, my father went to talk to the attorney about perhaps pulling strings to get me into Hopkins. At the time, Hopkins was an all-boys day school with only a few brick classroom buildings, but it was well-known as a very good college preparatory school.

At Hopkins, the required dress was a dress shirt with a jacket and tie, even a clip-on bowtie. Hopkins classes started in the 7th grade, or First Form, as they used to call it. I already missed 7th grade there, plus many of the young boys who went to Hopkins were from more culturally and educationally advanced parents than I had. In fact, some of them were sons of Yale professors. So, I started at a distinct disadvantage there. But the disadvantage went far beyond my family background. The Headmaster of Hopkins was evidently not too pleased with anyone going over his head to admit a student without his personal approval, especially one not having met the requisite test score. He held it against me all through my five years at Hopkins, never going out of his way to say hello to me or, more importantly, to provide any assistance or guidance to me when I was seeking to apply to colleges. He never did because he was such a prick!

I truly struggled the first year I was at Hopkins in the 8th grade and always seemed to be bogged down with a great deal of angst. I was asked to do homework that I had never seen before and been exposed to, such as analyzing poems. And I also had a problem trying to figure out how to do many math problems. I remember crying some nights at home because I didn't know what I was doing or what I was even supposed to do. My father sent me downstairs to see Uncle Bernie, who had at least gone to college for a year or so. He was always much more analytical than my father, and he at least helped me to deal somewhat with the subject matter. And he also gave me the inspiration to keep doing the work as well as I could. Although I did not do that well in my first year at Hopkins, I got by with passing grades.

In my second year at Hopkins, the 9th grade, I took Latin I, French I, Algebra I, English, and Biology. I learned my lessons better since I already had the experience of my first year there, knowing what was expected of me. I was fortunate to have good teachers, especially in Latin I and French I. With Latin I, I learned that much of our English language was derived from Latin. It helped me greatly in learning English reading comprehension and understanding sentence construction since the verb in Latin is usually found at the end of the sentence. But until Latin I, I had not really understood proper sentence structure with nouns, verbs, adjectives, adverbs, and other elements of a sentence. I owe much of my learning to Latin I. I also learned French very well, which enabled me to go onto advanced college-level French four years later when I entered college as a freshman.

Throughout my time at Hopkins, I really did okay, attaining placement in the middle of a smart class of about 55 juniors and seniors. However, I always fell just short of the Honor Roll due to receiving grades of C+ in the Math courses instead of B-. I was, oh, so close. But, as hard as I tried, I never could seem to solve the word problems well enough in Algebra II, which, of course, comprised some of the same questions as in the SATs in my junior and senior years. As usual, I did not test too well on those tests. Finishing in the middle of my class, together with SAT scores that were not good enough, didn't open me up to being accepted to the Ivy League college that I really wanted.

At Hopkins, I was required to play either intramural or interscholastic sports. In my sophomore year, I tried out for the football team. I was then five foot ten inches and 185 pounds. I was big enough but really a bit overweight and slow. Back in those days, our school didn't have a weight room, and we were not required to lift weights. I think weightlifting would have helped me lose some of my baby fat. I remember in mid-August running drills, trying out for the football team in the heat of late summer on the football field before the school year started. It was very difficult for me to get through that training period. I made the junior varsity, but mostly, only seniors started on the first team. The next summer, with more experience, I had proven I was ready to be one of the starting, first-team guards on offense and the nose tackle on defense. But a week before the first game in my junior year, my cleat caught in the grass during one of our football practices, and I dislocated my right knee for the second time in three years.

The first time I had done it, I was in the 9th grade playing pick-up basketball in my backyard when I dribbled in for a layup and unfortunately hit my right knee against the right concrete pillar of the middle bay of the garage. I had never experienced anything so painful in my life then or since as my kneecap (patella) being knocked out of its socket. I had to wait for my father to come home from work and take me to the closest hospital across the street from my Hebrew School. Approximately an hour after the incident happened, the orthopedic surgeon popped the patella back in place, and I was good to go. Except I had to be on crutches for almost two months because many ligaments and tendons that were displaced when the patella went awry needed to heal. So, when it happened again in September of my junior year after I had already won a starting position on both offense and defense, I was heartbroken. I had to wait until my senior year to get back on the football field. But by then, the head coach already had his misgivings about playing me due to my knee problems, and I was confined to being a back-up.

Perhaps my only claim to fame was in our final game, being put into the defensive lineup in a play against Kingswood School in West Hartford on a 4th down. I was so revved up that I burst through two players on the offensive line to block the punt, and we recovered the fumble. I was so happy I finally got to do something worthwhile for the team. But that was the end of my football career. I was terribly frustrated with never having been physically well-enough to play football because I liked the thrill of making good contact with an opponent, both blocking and tackling, working in tandem with teammates to make a successful play, and being resilient enough to even take a big hit from an opponent.

I made some wonderful friends at Hopkins, some of whom I still communicate with all these years later on social media and occasionally by telephone. But one of my best friends for life, from the time we were both toddlers, Michael W., died in May of 2022. Michael was very special to me and to all those who knew him. He was so intelligent and could keep a conversation going on almost any subject, especially sports. After Hopkins, he went to Yale College and then Harvard Law School. He had a very good career as the senior attorney at a leading casualty insurance company in Hartford. He loved the Baltimore Orioles and would have been so happy to see the team finally winning and in first place. He also loved UCONN women's basketball, and he went to several of their Final Four games over the years. I miss Michael a lot.

Well, after my graduation from Hopkins, when all the other students in my class had already received their admissions to Yale, Harvard, and other top schools, I still hadn't received notice of my admission to any college of my choice, largely due to the fact the Headmaster at Hopkins never tried to help me. I was fortunate that my father again had another acquaintance who knew a major benefactor at Colby College in Maine. He was the founder and owner of a major shoe company in Maine. My father and I met with him in July 1959 at the Insurance City Open Golf Tournament at the Wethersfield Country Club in Wethersfield, CT. We talked for a while out on the golf course there about Colby College and my aspirations, although I had never even been to Maine. He promised to put in a good word for me, and he did. I filed my application to the college sometime in July 1959. I also recall having met with a local Colby alumnus in or near Waterbury, CT, for an interview, and I learned of my acceptance sometime in August. I had no idea how cold it gets in Maine during the winter. But I was in, ready to go to work.

By then, I had already started up a bad habit of both of my parents: smoking cigarettes. I still don't know why

I ever started smoking over the summer between my graduation from high school and the beginning of college. Maybe I was nervous about beginning a new life away from home. But that bad habit lasted with me for about 15 years, smoking nearly a pack a day into my early thirties. It was a dangerous habit that could have taken my life already if I had not stopped in 1974 when I went to the funeral of a dear colleague at work who died of throat cancer after a two-year battle. I threw away my cigarettes that day and never went back. But I still have some after-effects to this day, with some occasional bronchitis.

In early September 1959, my father, mother, and I drove nearly six hours up to Waterville, ME. The campus was a short drive from the business district up on a big hill overlooking the town with a very picturesque view. It was a lovely campus with all buildings in harmony with brick colonial architecture. That day, I learned I had been assigned to a dormitory room with a classmate from Ireland. I met Frank later that day. He asked me to please wake him up whenever he had an early class in the morning. And I agreed. However, I might have been better off trying to wake up a sleeping bear because Frank was so very difficult to wake up. And he would even get upset at me when I tried to wake him up. I remember one night after midnight, while I was sleeping, Frank must have been up studying when he suddenly started yelling something about a mouse in the room. I then woke up, and we both tried to defeat the mouse for well over another half hour before it was finally subdued. Fortunately, the rest of my freshman year with Frank went fine, and my grades were satisfactory based on my good private school background.

I rushed for a fraternity in my sophomore year and was accepted. And the hazing proved to be somewhat challenging. One of my assigned tasks was to thumb a ride from the campus in Maine to Boston's train station and sleep on a bench there overnight with the homeless. And I did so. There were undoubtedly other lesser, menial tasks that I cannot recall now. But the final task for initiation was standing on a Sunday for eight hours blind-folded in a room with other pledges listening to an off-key female opera singer ruin an operetta song. It was apparently designed to be a major test of steadfastness and endurance in the face of psychological adversity. And we all passed.

I became a history major because I enjoyed history. But I had proceeded on a rather tenuous premise that I would seek to become a doctor in accordance with my father's wishes. So, I took all the required pre-Med courses in biology, inorganic chemistry, organic chemistry, and physics. Some of them even twice. I remember the first day in my inorganic chemistry class, the professor threateningly said, "look to your left and look to your right; many of you will not be here for the second semester." And I was one of them.

During the many decades since then, I have never forgotten what he said, especially when the college alumni office has continued to send me many letters each year requesting more and more donations. At the time, one of my roommates in the fraternity house majored in Economics and went on to get his advanced degree in Economics at Princeton University before having a successful career working for our US State Department. My other roommate majored in Business Administration, and he attended the Harvard Business School before creating a successful company of children's clothing and furnishings that he later sold for many millions of dollars. They had both implored me not to take physics and inorganic chemistry in the same semester. But I foolishly did not listen to them. I failed both, although I took the courses again in summer school and received much better grades. However, the writing was on the wall for me, and the pre-med courses proved to be too overwhelming for me to even apply to medical school. Therefore, I began to consider a different career.

I took the LSAT law boards in the fall of my senior year. But, as with all my previous testing, the results were not very good. So, I thought about becoming a history teacher. One day in late August 1963, a few guys my age I knew from around the city stopped by near the end of the furniture store's fire sale, looking for end tables. I spoke to them about what they were up to, and they said they were entering law school in Boston at Suffolk Law School. I thought about it for a few days and decided why I shouldn't go to law school, too. I told my parents, then packed up my little beige 1957 VW Beetle that my father had purchased for me after college and headed for Boston.

This is a true story, not fiction. At the time, Suffolk University and its law school were located all in one building on Derne Street on Beacon Hill in Boston. I called my fraternity father from college, Dick G., then living near there and attending another law school down the street from Suffolk, to ask if I could stay with him for a few nights. Over the weekend, we talked about my going to law school, and I agreed that it would be better for me than becoming a history teacher. Then, on Monday morning in early September 1963, I drove over to Suffolk Law School and found a parking space on Beacon Hill, which was very tricky because parking there is very difficult to find. I went into the admissions office and asked if I could go to law school when it opened in a few days. The woman asked me if I had taken the law boards, and she also asked where I went to college. Fortunately, another fraternity brother of mine from Colby was already set to enter his second year at law school there, so my college credentials were not totally unknown. I called to ask that my LSAT score be sent over to the law school. And then, I was admitted to law school a few days later.

That first day at law school, I met two classmates who also had just met each other and were looking for another roommate. One had graduated from Providence University, and the other from Saint Mary's in Halifax, Nova Scotia. We started looking for an apartment together and found what seemed like a somewhat new three-bedroom apartment with off-street parking in Allston, not too far from "the T" subway on Commonwealth Avenue. We all got along well, taking turns driving to school, and we had the beginning of a pleasant first year there. But then there was the tragic assassination of our beloved President Kennedy in November 1963. That entire weekend, we sat transfixed in front of the TV, watching the horrible news.

Most of the time, we studied our law books in torts, criminal law, civil procedure, property law, and contracts. I did fine, although I really do not remember whether my roommates also passed. I didn't remember seeing either of them after that first year.

For my second year, I had two new roommates, and we lived together in an old apartment building in Brighton, the front door of which faced the parking lot of a big supermarket. One roommate was a fellow law school classmate named Peter M. from Woonsocket, RI, and the other was a friend of his who was a dental student in Boston. We all got along well, sharing dinners together and being respectful of each other's space.

In my final year, Peter and I decided to room together again. We found a second-floor apartment in an old house in Brookline owned by an older Italian couple who had evidently remodeled the second floor of their home to obtain rental income. The house was situated up a narrow, winding street from "the T" on Beacon Street, less than a mile from where our previous Brighton apartment was located. Later, I learned the elderly man who owned the house used to ride the "T" into Boston to buy anise oil to make his own anisette liqueur. Occasionally, he'd share some of it with us. And it was superb.

Even before our classes began, a fellow law school classmate and I met and took a stroll down to the junction of Commonwealth Avenue and Beacon Street near

Boston University. He recognized a young woman who was walking together with another young woman. When he stopped to say hello to his female acquaintance, I started talking to the other woman. She told me it was her first day in Boston and that she had just transferred to Boston University from the State University at Buffalo. She was an attractive, petite woman with short, dark hair. Her name was strange. At first, I thought she said it was Irma. But, no, it was "Irva."

She and I started dating, and then it became quite often. It later became somewhat serious, and I drove up to see her at her home in Monroe, New York, over the Thanksgiving weekend and then again later during Christmas vacation. I was 24, and she was just 21. Her parents operated a bungalow colony for summer guests and a children's day camp on several acres of land that were owned by

Irva's mother, her two uncles, and her grandmother. Her grandfather, Barnett, had already passed away. Her father, Jack, appeared to be a hardworking man with not much hair who usually drove around on a tractor during the day cutting the grass there, and he also took care of all the necessary maintenance chores. His wife, Marilyn, whom everyone called "Min," seemed to be an intelligent woman who stayed mostly in the house, taking care of the books for the businesses and caring for Irva's younger sister, Harma. Plus, she served on the local Monroe school board. Min's father and mother had started out in Cleveland, Ohio, with a construction company there. But years later, they decided to move with Min and her two brothers to buy several big parcels of land in Monroe, New York, that would become their home sites next to, and across the street from, each other, in addition to the many acres of land used for their business properties. It seemed like a very close-knit family compound.

Irva and I became engaged and then later got married on February 20, 1966, at a local restaurant in Monroe, NY, that served perhaps up to 100 sit-down guests for our wedding. Being that we only had a long weekend for a honeymoon, we went to a nearby resort hotel in the Catskill Mountains. When we returned to Boston, my roommate Peter agreed to move to another room in the house. Across the hall from us was another married classmate, Gerard D., who years later would become a noted criminal lawyer in Rockland County, NY. This period in history was marked by an increase in hostilities during the height of the Vietnam War, and it seemed like young men were either enlisting in large numbers or fleeing the draft to Canada. But I got married instead. In the Spring, my studying significantly increased when I'd drive from Boston to Hartford, CT, every Saturday with one or two other law students in the area to take the Connecticut Bar Review course. At that time, Massachusetts law was often cited as a minority law position different from many other States, including Connecticut. I, therefore, had to brush up on the prevailing law in Connecticut.

I graduated from law school in June and began another Connecticut Bar Review course in New Haven at Yale Law School. I took the Connecticut Bar Exam in July 1966 and received notice about a month later that I had passed. Just prior to that time, Irva and I had already rented a clean, walk-up, two-bedroom apartment in a pleasant neighborhood in New Haven, not far from Southern Connecticut State College. Soon after, we learned that Irva was pregnant and due for delivery in February 1967. I then had to decide what to do with my life. My father had another acquaintance who knew a certain tax attorney in a law firm in downtown New Haven.

I called the law firm and scheduled an appointment for an interview with the attorney who was one of the three law partners, one older and one younger than him. To be perfectly honest, I had never really thought about taxation as a career since l had left law school with only a basic individual income tax course and an estate and gift taxation course. I met with the attorney and inquired about the open position, which was to do tax research and write opinions analyzing tax issues in cases the firm would be handling. I received a telephone call a few weeks later that I would be hired at an annual salary of $5,000. Yes, that's right. No mistake. It was 1966.

Winter came, and we purchased a crib, carriage, and other things for the baby. At the time, there were no such things as disposable diapers. There were only laundry services that would pick up the smelly diapers, launder them, and then deliver clean ones the next week. Sunday, February 5, 1967, was a very mild day for that time of year in Connecticut. But soon after it began, Irva started to receive a few contractions, which continued in intensity for most of the afternoon. Finally, before nightfall, her doctor called to suggest she go to the hospital. At that time, hospitals did not allow husbands to be in the delivery rooms when babies were born. Therefore, I never got to see the delivery of my beautiful baby girl, named Geri, a few hours later. But the next day was truly memorable. It started to snow lightly in the morning, and it continued to pile up all morning.

Visiting hours at the time started at 11:00 am. By that time, there were several inches of snow on the ground. So, driving on the major roads was not good. I think it may have taken me almost an hour and one-half to drive a distance to the hospital that would have normally taken me about 20 minutes or so in good weather. But when I finally got there, I was so enthralled just watching my baby girl, realizing I had become a father to this beautiful little one. I congratulated Irva and kissed her for her good work.

By this time, I had been in the law firm for several months. It was enough time for me to realize my shortcomings in not having enough tax education to do a better job. So, I made up my mind to seek further education in tax law. I applied to three or four law schools offering a Master of Laws degree in taxation or LLM. Because my daughter would be crawling by the time my schooling would start, I thought going to the University of Miami School of Law would be better for all of us than going to the law school at Washington University in St. Louis or in other cities where winters can be very difficult. After my admittance to the University of Miami School of Law, I flew down by myself to look for an apartment to rent.

I was fortunate that my Aunt Harriet had a cousin married to a dentist who lived in Miami, and she showed me around to different rental listings in her air-conditioned car because I had stupidly rented a car without air conditioning. I'll never forget what a terrific woman she was to help me like she did. In fact, both she and her husband were two of the most wonderful people I ever met.

I rented a clean, rather basic, garden apartment in South Miami, a relatively short 10 to 15-minute ride across the railroad tracks to Coral Gables, where the University of Miami School of Law was located. My classes were all in the evening. Accordingly, I would study most weekdays in our air-conditioned bedroom while Irva watched Geri crawling about both inside and on the grass outside in the sunny weather.

Before Thanksgiving, tests confirmed that I had unfortunately managed to get an ulcer from studying so much and drinking too much grapefruit juice and coffee. After consulting with a doctor at the hospital, I changed my diet and was able to get rid of the ulcer just as fast as I had gotten it. Otherwise, I had a very productive year learning the tax courses, which would provide me with a good foundation for a long career in taxation. In retrospect, I think my decision to attend the law school at the University of Miami for my LLM was a good move on my part because it is a fine law school with good, dedicated teachers.

My Work

From the time I was 15, I worked mostly every summer. My first job was stocking shelves and bagging groceries at a supermarket in West Haven, CT, which required me to take two buses each way to and from work. The first bus I took was to downtown New Haven, and the second one was from there to Campbell Avenue in the center of West Haven. Roundtrip, it took at least two hours or more of each day for travel time.

When I was 16 in the summer of 1958, I mostly caddied on the golf course at The Woodbridge Country Club. To get there, I either hitched a ride with someone I knew from New Haven or borrowed my mother's car after I got my driver's license. It was a second-hand, 1954, two-door, two-tone green Pontiac with a stick shift. In fact, I learned to drive using this car. After arriving at the country club, I would seek out the caddy-master to find out if I could carry the bags of two golfers. At the time, golf carts were not yet used at all, and the going rate for a caddy there was $4 per bag for 18 holes. And most golfers had very heavy bags. So, after a long day carrying two heavy golf bags, I earned a whopping $8 for the day. I caddied for anyone I could. Some men or women I had met before. Others were new to me. I did it for a few months that summer, which helped me to buy clothes for school. I learned a lot about human nature watching other people grapple with hitting the little white ball and the various human reactions to hitting it well and not too well.

At 17, I got a summer job through the son of one of the owners of the local "Cott" soda bottling plant, whom I had known well. My job was to put the cases of empty soda bottles on the conveyor belt that would take the bottles through to the washing machines. At the time, I remember the hourly rate was nearly $2.50, which was quite good for 1959. The big guy across the way from me had the job of putting the cases of full bottles on the conveyor belt that would take them to the site where they would be ready for shipment. In mid-August, my mother came by one day to pick me up from work, and she was a bit aghast at what I was doing for eight hours every day.

During the following two summers, at ages 18 and 19, I was already in college. I may have worked part-time somewhere, but I needed to take summer courses in Inorganic Chemistry and Physics at the University of Connecticut-Waterbury to make up for my failed grades in those subjects at Colby. At 20, I needed to fulfill a math requirement, so I took a summer course in trigonometry, which was given in the evenings at the University of New Haven. In the mornings, I had gotten a job picking up garbage for the City of New Haven. I would get up at about 4:30 a.m. each weekday morning, have a quick breakfast, and take a bus downtown to be at work at 5:30 a.m. I rode the garbage truck on its route through downtown New Haven for at least five hours and then was able to get off work by 11:00 am so I could study my Trigonometry course assignments.

By this time, my mother had a new second-hand car. It was a 1957 beige Rambler station wagon, also a stick shift. Following my first year in law school, during the summer of 1964, I asked my parents if I could use my mother's car to drive across the country to California and work there for the summer. They said fine. I managed to find three passengers to go with me to help pay for gas and tolls. One was a classmate from law school, and the other two were women at other schools in Boston who found my notice on their bulletin boards seeking passengers wishing to travel to California.

We set off early Monday morning in the second week of June and made it as far as Warren, Ohio. We found a motel and split up into two rooms. On the second day, we traveled over 700 miles to Ames, Iowa. Again, we found a motel to stay in. On the third day, we limped into a motel in Cheyenne, Wyoming. On the night of the fourth day, we arrived in San Francisco, California. It was an arduous journey of nearly 3,000 miles in four days, but I think we all felt it would be. At that point, we split up after having a beer together at a bar downtown.

One of the highlights of our trip was taking a side trip from Warren, Ohio, to South Bend, Indiana, to visit the campus of the University of Notre Dame at the urging of my law school classmate. We saw the always recognizable Golden Dome that sits atop a historical landmark building there. In addition, we took the time to enter the famous college football stadium there. It was a magical place to see the beautiful, lush, deep green grass on the field that, in September, would be torn up by the football cleats of many college players. Another highlight was stopping the car in scenic Wyoming to see the wondrous vistas of mountains filled with endless trees overlooking a long, wide river. It was one of the most picturesque scenes I ever took with my old camera.

After spending at least four days visiting with my aunt and uncle and my two cousins in San Mateo, California, I drove the eight-plus hours to Los Angeles. I went to visit my fraternity father from college, Dick G., who had rented an apartment for the summer in Hollywood, CA. As I recall, the apartment building and its small pool were situated on a rather narrow, vertical piece of property down the street from Grauman's Chinese Theatre in Hollywood. Dick G.'s father owned retail gasoline and convenience stores in Massachusetts and throughout New England. As a result, Dick G. got a job for the summer in a suit and tie with the then Tidewater Oil Company, later known as Getty Oil, on Wilshire Boulevard in Los Angeles, which was owned by billionaire John Paul Getty.

Dick helped me get a job for the summer in the mailroom of the company he worked for. It was not a very interesting job for someone going to law school, but it helped me pay my share of the rent, gasoline, and other costs while I stayed with Dick until the middle of August 1964. On the weekends we had fun in greater Los Angeles, going to the beach in Malibu, visiting Disneyland, going to Dodger Stadium to see the Dodgers play against their rival, the San Francisco Giants, listening to the music of Johnny Rivers and his band at the "Whiskey A Go Go" on Sunset Boulevard in West Hollywood, going over to see the campus of UCLA in Westwood, and even just going out to dinner around the city, where we saw movie stars like Tuesday Weld.

I then started my trip back across the country, driving first towards Las Vegas, NV. But the normally short trip was turned into a nightmare because my mother's car broke down on the outskirts of Barstow, CA, in the Mohave Desert. The car had to be towed from the desert back to the only gas station there. Evidently, the rapid cross-country trip in June was too much for the old car. I called my father and told him the bad news, and he authorized the gas station to fix it. But the engine was completely taken apart at least twice and rebuilt to get it to run properly. Finally, after the fifth day, I was able to start driving again to Las Vegas.

I finally arrived in Las Vegas and stayed at The Sands Hotel. I was only there for a few days, but I got to see a performance by a young comedian named Don Rickles in one of the bars there, rather than in a big venue reserved for a recognized star. I just happened to sit at the bar next to another young man who struck up a conversation with me after the performance. He asked me if I wanted to go see a certain performer at another hotel. Without thinking, I said sure. So, we got in his car, and before we left the parking lot, he propositioned me. I told him, "sorry, I'm straight, not gay." And then I got out of the car and went back to the hotel. I think I only lost $50 that night at the "21 table." The problem was that I had lost it in less than 20 minutes because I was never much of a gambler.

The next day, I started my trek home by myself with no passengers. Unlike the trip to California, which took a northern route, I now took a southern route on Rte.66. I tried not to push it, given what happened to the engine on the rushed trip going to California. But I was still making good time until I hit Wheeling, West Virginia, where the engine stopped working, and again, I had to call my father and tell him the unfortunate news. This time, I only had to spend a few nights in Wheeling, which was a good thing because there was not much for me to do there. By this time, my father had already spent over three hundred dollars to fix the engine. But undoubtedly, it would cost at least a few hundred more now. Again, my father showed me a great deal of tolerance for having to spend so much to fix the car. I estimated the costs to fix the engine may have totaled over $500 in both Barstow and Wheeling. But I managed to make it home to New Haven without further costs. My father soon after sold that car.

The summer of 1965 was one of my favorites. However, it started out in a rather disappointing manner. I was hired by a company in Boston to paint a gas station with a few other men. I remember being there for perhaps not even a full day, and I was told to go home because I did not paint fast enough. Maybe I was a bit too meticulous. When I got back to my apartment, I was somewhat down for not being good enough to keep my job as a painter for even a full day. But then I received a call later from my father telling me I had gotten a job as a summer intern in Washington, D.C., to work for my Congressman Bob Giaimo from the 3rd Congressional District of Connecticut, which included New Haven and its suburbs of West Haven, Orange, Milford, Hamden, Woodbridge, North Haven, Wallingford, and several others.

I was so happy and grateful to the leader of the Democratic Party in New Haven for doing this for me. It wasn't at all about the pay but rather the honor of working in Washington for such a good and decent congressman and doing analytical work for him, which meant a lot to me.

He was a tall, nice-looking Italian man, the son of an immigrant from Sicily, who was politically astute enough to be able to serve for eleven consecutive two-year terms. When I arrived at his Congressional office, he asked me to be his legislative intern, serving under his Legislative Director, who advised him on all legislative policy areas and assisted in the development of policy positions and legislative initiatives. I thoroughly enjoyed analyzing pieces of proposed legislation and writing opinion letters on them. I also wrote many letters signed by the Congressman that were sent to his constituents in response to their letters to the Congressman. I was pleased that the Congressman appreciated my work well enough to refrain from editing/redoing the letters. I think he and I shared the same political views to seek to stamp out poverty and racial injustice. The summer of 1965 was indeed a special time in our country's history because of the "Great Society" domestic programs launched by President Lyndon B. Johnson. I also got to see those pieces of legislation first-hand while working for Congressman.

As previously noted, in the summer of 1966, I was totally immersed in studying for the Connecticut Bar Exam.

In the summer of 1967, when I returned from Florida with my wife and daughter, I was still awaiting the results of my applications for jobs in taxation. So, I got an interim job working for the Clerk of the Superior Court, responding to motions filed in the Court cases. However, I found the work far more interesting when I was able to see lawyers plead their cases before juries in the courtroom. I was fortunate to see who the best trial lawyers were in the area. A month or two later, I received an acceptance letter to work in the tax accounting department of Price Waterhouse & Co. in New York, which at the time was in lower Manhattan on Broad Street.

Working for an accounting firm was not my preference, but I viewed it as a stepping stone to a better job in tax law. We moved to an apartment in North Yonkers, NY, and I commuted to Grand Central Station by train every day. Then, I had to take the Lexington Avenue subway down to the Wall Street area. I hated most everything about the commute to and from this job, especially having to take a crowded Lexington Avenue subway during the summer, with terrible body odor all around me. But that was not the fault of Price Waterhouse & Co. because I enjoyed the tax work. But there was too much wasted time just traveling to and from the job. At the time, and maybe even today, Price Waterhouse & Co. also had an accounting policy that required all tax accountants, even tax attorneys, to work on financial accounting audits. But I simply did not like audits and did not see myself at all cut out for doing them.

I was first asked to count cash and then record accounts receivable. Six months passed, and I had already applied for other jobs. One that came through for me a few months later was a job as a tax attorney for a Fortune 500 company that had just moved from Park Avenue in Manhattan to Stamford, Connecticut. I jumped at it. The pay was only a little better, but at the time, Connecticut didn't have an income tax, so my net spendable income would go up because it would no longer be subject to the

New York City and New York State income withholding taxes. In addition, in a position as a Tax Attorney, the legal nature of the tax work was just what I wanted.

Then Irva and I moved again back to live in Orange, Connecticut, a suburb of New Haven. At the time, homes in Stamford, which is in Fairfield County, were and still are much more expensive than in towns like Orange in New Haven County. So now I had to commute by car from Orange to Stamford, an hour or so each way on the Merritt Parkway. The corporate headquarters was located at 120 Long Ridge Road in a modern multilevel building not too far from the Stamford exit. Attached to the building was an ample garage for employee parking.

In my early years there, my work entailed mostly compliance with sections of the Internal Revenue Code containing the requirements for accomplishing tax-free mergers and acquisitions. Then, in 1974, the VP of Taxes who hired me, Wallace C., asked me to oversee the new federal laws embodied in the Employee Retirement Income Security Act (ERISA), that set forth the minimum standards for compliance by employee benefit plans, including defined benefit and defined contribution plans, in private industry. Then, in later years, I was involved to a greater extent in seeking to restructure the company's foreign operations to reduce exposure to both US and international taxation. After I had been working at the corporation for over ten years, my boss, Wallace C., unfortunately, died of a sudden heart attack well before his normal retirement date, which apparently may have been precipitated by top executives pushing him too hard. On and after his funeral, I met and became acquainted with his widow and daughter. In fact, his daughter dated my friend, Steve D., for a while. But she later ended up marrying a noted plastic surgeon whose practice was then located in Scarsdale, NY.

I enjoyed my fourteen years working for the corporation in Stamford. But more than anything, I enjoyed the people I worked with and for. They were all very diligent, productive tax law and tax accounting professionals who all got along very well together. You don't usually find that in just any workplace. In fact, one of my work colleagues and my closest friend there was Kent A., with whom I enjoyed playing racquetball at the local Stamford YMCA one night each week after work. We played for at least a few or more years, and I don't remember much about our games except the one night I mistakenly got too close to his right-handed backhand, and his racquet clipped the eyebrow over my left eye. After seeing blood, we quickly showered and went over to the Stamford Hospital, where a young surgeon put stitches in my eyebrow.

I always had an edge playing racquetball with Kent because I was many years younger than him. But he didn't care. We had a special comradery together that enabled me to appreciate his exceptional goodness as a human being. He was one of the most likable, good men I ever met. Men like Kent are so rare because he was so patient with those he worked with and never raised his voice in anger to anyone in the more than twenty years that I knew him. He and his wonderful wife, Maria, invited me to join them for Christmas dinners probably fifteen years after we had both already left the company in Stamford.

After we were married, Jeri joined me in visiting their happy home in Milford for Christmas dinner at least twice. Maria had no false pretenses, which was a quality that Kent also shared with her. He always went out of his way to help a colleague or friend who needed advice on how to fix something at home. He was a handyman whose major interest, outside of his wife and two sons, Scott and Bruce, was sailing his boat on Long Island Sound. As I sit here thinking about them, one of my greatest regrets in life was losing contact with these wonderful people several years ago when we were still living in Avon, CT, and Jeri first started the onset of her MS in 2004. Now, I have learned from searching the Internet that Maria passed away in 2013 at the age of 85, and Kent was apparently last known to have died at 89 on February 11,

2017.

In 1983, my fourteenth year working at the company in Stamford, I began to see the early beginnings of what we now see so prevalent in so many big corporations today: executives at the top getting the lion's share of the compensation and not enough of the compensation trickling down to the middle and lower management rungs of corporations. When I had finally had enough of what I still perceive today as a terribly misguided policy, I left the corporation towards the end of 1983. I had no other job, so I decided to open my own practice of tax law in Westport, CT, where I lived. It was a major move for me to leave the company I had worked at for so long. But the company graciously offered me a severance package for several months.

I rented an office in Westport in the lower level of a law firm that specialized in domestic relations law. It was a very nice office, but much too big and too expensive for my needs. In hindsight, of course, I probably should have first just worked from home because the rent I had to pay gouged me so much during that first year, getting me deep into debt. I joined the Westport Rotary Club and became a Certified Financial Planner. I made guest speaker presentations in front of the Westport Rotary Club and the Norwalk Business and Professional Women's Club on tax subjects of interest to the members. The Rotary members were mostly professionals like me, as well as others who owned or operated local businesses. I enjoyed my time in the Westport Rotary Club because the members were very cordial. And I made several business acquaintances there. In fact, a former President of the Westport Rotary Club, Stan A., officiated at my wedding to my second wife.

I never had enough clients. However, I did have one major client who gave me a very modest retainer for all the work I would have to put in. But I needed the money. I sued the federal government in a US District Court tax case regarding the client's Defined Benefit Plan, which purchased securities on margin that "contributed importantly" to the accomplishment of its tax-exempt purpose. The federal government's position was that the client's margin securities were "debt-financed property" under IRC Section 514(b)(1), causing the creation of unrelated business taxable income under IRC Section 511. I filed a Brief plus a Reply Brief with the US District Court for the Southern District of Florida, which took many hours and days to complete. I argued the case in front of the US District Court judge in Sarasota, FL. To this day, I still believe the case should have been decided in favor of my client. But it was not. I lost.

By the time the case was heard, I had already moved the office to my home, which was just as easily accessible to clients who visited me as the rented office was and was far less expensive. I practiced law there for probably another year or so. Then, I needed money to pay my mounting bills.

I decided to supplement my law practice by getting my real estate license in Connecticut. I took the required course and passed. I also initially joined a local real estate office to sell homes. Soon after, I took a commercial real estate course to learn how to value commercial real estate, including office buildings, shopping centers, and others. I also obtained my broker's license to pursue more commercial real estate sales. I was very diligent, but nothing I did ever seemed to be enough to be successful. I think that throughout the time I was in my home office, I may have sold one home and maybe a small piece of commercial real estate.

I remember working hard to find a location in Bridgeport, CT, for the first "Costco" to come into our area of Connecticut as well as the "The Home Depot." But I couldn't compete with the bigger commercial real estate companies. This was already late in 1988-89. And I was considering going in another direction with my life. But before I did, I took my daughter, Geri, with me to the

National Real Estate Convention held in Honolulu, HI. I think she had fun spending time with me on Waikiki Beach in front of our hotel. One day, I rented a jeep and took her all over the island of Oahu to see Pearl Harbor, the Dole pineapple plantations, and the different towns along the way. It was great fun.

In early January 1990, I rented my house in Westport to a man I knew well from the Westport Rotary Club, and I moved to Jupiter, Florida, to study for the Florida Bar Exam to be held in July. I rented a very nice two-bedroom apartment on the first floor of a short, high-rise building there near Route 1. I also leased a new Honda Civic from a nearby car dealer. To pay my bills, I got a job for four and half months as counsel to a small aircraft trading company in Jupiter that brokered and bought and sold corporate jets around the country. The owner of the company was a good old boy from Texas who was probably one of the most bigoted individuals I have ever met. I think he never suspected I was Jewish. Or, if he did, he never let on? But he agreed to pay me an annual salary of $40,000 during the day while I studied more than twenty video cassette tape presentations of Florida Law and Federal constitutional case law at night after work.

My work as counsel to the company was somewhat interesting because I had never been exposed to the airplane business. I remember drafting agreements for the purchase and sale and/or brokerage of the purchase and sale of corporate jets. The owner also asked me to draw up agreements with the architect and the builder of a large mansion he was interested in building right next to the intercoastal waterway in Jupiter, neither of which I had ever done before. I forget now how large the home was supposed to be. But it was extremely large for just two people, even if their two sons lived there with them.

At the end of my study for the Florida Bar, I had to take two days off from work to fly to Tampa, FL, to get a hotel room and take the Florida Bar Exam, which was given in July over a two-day period in its Convention Center in downtown Tampa. But I never told the owner of the business why I was taking off Thursday and Friday. On the first day of the Exam, I vividly remember walking into the Convention Center on a Thursday morning in the third week of July 1990 with as many, or even more, women than men. This was such a major difference from twenty-four years earlier, in 1966, when I had taken the Connecticut Bar Exam with only a few scattered women among the many hundreds of men sitting for the Exam.

I went back to work on the Monday following the Florida Bar Exam, and the owner questioned me why I had taken off two straight days for the only time in the four and half months I worked there. I admitted to him I had taken the Florida Bar Exam, and he went ballistic, screaming at me, yelling, "How dare you?" and the like. After a short while, he came back and fired me on the spot. He expressed to me that my taking the exam meant to him that I was interested in finding a better job in law. Of course, I denied that, but then I left the office without further discussion.

I went back to my apartment, packed up my belongings, and took my leased Honda Civic back to the dealer. The next day, I went to the airport in West Palm Beach and took a flight to New York. Since my house in Westport was rented, I could not live there. I called a friend for a suggestion, and he recommended I call a female friend of his who might let me rent a room in her house in Fairfield, CT. I also knew her and always had a good relationship with her. She agreed to allow me to rent a bedroom in her house for a reasonable monthly amount. So here I was at a relatively low point in my life, without a job, living in someone else's house, and being unhappy with my lot in life. In the early autumn of 1990, I decided to get serious about applying for a good job.

I filled out an application to the State of Connecticut for a position as a tax attorney. I have heard nothing back from the state for several months. In the meantime, I had to find something to do. I called Manpower to get any job I could. A week or so later, I got a call that I would be hired to do door-to-door distribution of a flyer to local businesses in a particular commercial area nearby. That meant being on foot doing a mindless task a robot could do. By that time, it was almost near the end of the year, during which time I continued to contact the State of Connecticut regarding my application. Again, I heard nothing. Finally, I received a letter in January 1991 from the Director of the Tax Department in the Connecticut Department of Revenue Services (DRS) offering me an interview in early February.

Soon thereafter, the Connecticut legislature enacted the state's first income tax in 1991 under then-Governor Lowell Weicker. He also extended to two Connecticut native tribal nations, the Mashantucket Pequot Indians and the Mohegan Indians, the lucrative rights to open and monopolize gambling casinos on their reservations in the State.

I was very much against the governor's State income tax because I thought it would hurt the attraction of new businesses to Connecticut, disincentivize families from moving to Connecticut, and impose an undue financial burden on Connecticut residents. I was also very much against the governor giving the tribal nations such a big windfall at the expense of the State, which would receive only 25% of the slot machine revenue. In retrospect, I believe the State income tax has not helped Connecticut as much as the governor may have thought it would, and I believe he could have also pursued other alternative revenue sources for the State, including allowing it to compete with the tribal nations with State-owned casinos in other locations in the State. But he didn't. Given that he recently died, I don't wish to disparage the former governor further. But suffice it to say, I did not agree with very much of what he did in 1991.

In February, I drove to Hartford for my interview at DRS, which took nearly an hour from Fairfield by car. I met with an extremely nice gentleman named Albert S., the Director of Tax for DRS, who gave me more than enough time to review my resume with him and let me tell him about my background in tax law. He seemed like such a good, kind man that I hoped I would be accepted for the job. Within a few days, I received a telephone call advising me that I would be hired on an interim basis. What I didn't know at the time, but learned several months later, was the only reason for the opening in the Department for that position was because the lawyer who previously held the position had opted to leave for what he thought would be a better job for himself.

As it turned out, that job was not what he thought it would be, and so a few months later, he tried to get his former position back. But, by then, my job performance was already highly regarded. I took to the job very well, using my background in estate and gift tax law to review DRS files on decedents' estates and write letters to their attorneys asking for further information to determine their level of compliance with the values of properties they reported on the estate and gift tax returns, as well as the amounts they excluded from taxation.

After a year's time in the position working under Al, I had to reapply for a permanent position in the department based on the fact the State still regarded me as being in an interim position. Fortunately, I was rehired as a permanent employee of the department, where I remained for the next nineteen years until my retirement on June 30, 2011. Unfortunately, Al took early retirement before the beginning of 1993, and I did not have the opportunity to work under him any longer. But I did have a long, continuing relationship with him right up until 2022, when I last spoke to him by telephone and sent him a Christmas card.

During the many earlier years of Al's retirement, Robert E., another attorney in our department, and I would meet with Al for lunch on several occasions. We also attended the funeral of his wife, who we learned had been separated from him. Now, his telephone is no longer in operation in New Britain, where he lived, so he may now either be living with his daughter or in an assisted living facility, or perhaps even have passed away. I miss speaking with him.

My legal position did, however, change over the years, from just reviewing estate and gift tax files, to also reviewing corporate tax cases in which multinational corporations used various tax avoidance methods to reduce or eliminate taxation: for example, by using a shell company subsidiary without any assets in Connecticut to transact business in order to avoid the Connecticut Corporation Income Tax, or by using unrealistic values on various intercompany purchase and sale transactions, or undertaking loan transactions between an out-of-State parent company and a subsidiary incorporated in Connecticut that minimize the amounts subject to taxation by the State of Connecticut, or by using a shell company subsidiary located in a tax haven like the Cayman Islands to hold its intangible assets and charge royalties to an operating subsidiary in Connecticut to reduce its tax liability in Connecticut by means of the deductions for royalties paid that were never taxed to the tax haven subsidiary.

I was tasked with reviewing these transactions, which were usually ferreted out by the department's tax auditors to issue fair and reasonable tax deficiencies. I recall that the largest corporation tax deficiency I had a hand in helping to issue was imposed on a well-known US multinational company in the approximate amount of $28 million. What made this particularly satisfying to me was, after I did extensive research on the company's own Internet Website, I learned so much valuable information about how it conducted its US and overseas operations that it felt compelled to pay the tax bill without ever contesting it in a lawsuit. It was probably the only case I ever had like that. But, the higher-ups I worked for at DRS never seemed to show any appreciation for me or anyone else doing such good work bringing in such a large amount of tax revenue for the citizens of Connecticut. I even advised an Assistant Commissioner about my work helping to bring in a Twenty-Eight Million Dollar check, and all he said was, "That's nice," without ever saying anything else. In fact, a few years later, that very same DRS executive brought a frivolous complaint against me for a spurious issue that required me to hire a criminal attorney and cost me a substantial out-of-pocket fine.

The bottom line is no one at DRS or the State Government ever personally acknowledged or thanked me for a job well done. Most of those top echelon officials at DRS were, and likely still are, part of the problem of many in the Connecticut State government who are just happy to get a good paycheck and future large pensions but don't wish to themselves engage in the work necessary to succeed for the Connecticut taxpayers who paid them their much larger compensation than mine.

My principal estate and gift tax review in the later years I was at DRS revolved around reviewing large estates that claimed the decedent died domiciled in Florida, where there is no estate and gift tax, rather than in Connecticut and most other States where such taxes exist. I'm only talking now about the very large estates at that time with assets valued at more than $12 million. Smaller estates have a federal tax exemption anyway, so only the estates of multimillionaires and billionaires were subject to my review. I had some success in prevailing on estates to settle some large cases based on the weight of evidence with many facts in favor of the State issuing the deficiency. After twenty years working for DRS, I had had enough of the "mickey-mouse BS" most of us employees had to put up with from the top executives there, and I retired to Florida because of my wife's illness, the weather and the prohibition in the Florida Constitution against a tax upon estates, inheritances or income of residents or citizens of the State.

I like not having my income subject to State taxation, so I can have more net spendable income to do with as I wish. However, Florida is really a state that is more suitable for wealthy "snowbirds" who have other residences up north during the summer when the heat in Florida can become unbearable. But another issue quite unbearable in Florida is the corrupt Republican politicians leading the State who continue to deceive and even tyrannize so many millions of Floridians who really have no one representing their best interests because the Democratic politicians lack the power to make the changes needed to make it a better State for middle-and-low-income classes to live in. I point to the failures of the Republican-led Florida legislature to prevent property and casualty insurance companies from excessively overcharging Florida residents for their homeowners and auto insurance coverages, as well as imposing on pregnant women unreasonable, heinous restrictions on abortions that violate their rights to privacy under the Florida Constitution.

I made many lifetime friends of mine at DRS: Albert S., Armida C., Fred C., Dorothy L., Robert E., Las W., John S., Jean M., John K., Felicia H., Holly W., Ernest A., Margaret (Peggy) J., Charles F., Shawn S., Jessica S., Shirley T., Nancy M., Kelli S., Anna C., Sarah K., Tommy S., Jack B., Mike G. Some were fellow attorneys and others were colleagues in other departments. This is a terrific group of individuals with whom I mostly interacted daily. I miss seeing them in person. But I still communicate with several of them on social media.

My Personal Life

As a youngster, I enjoyed playing sports with my friends, whether it was stickball behind the Finast Supermarket, basketball in my backyard, or football up the street at Edgewood Park. I played these sports with Tommy S., Barry K., Norman P., Stuie G., Joel B., and several others. I also recall that boys in our grammar school once played a football game against boys from another local grammar school with real helmets and shoulder pads on in the open field adjacent to the bridge on Chapel Street leading to the Yale Bowl, which was less than a half-mile from where we lived. We got beat. On one play, I was on the sidelines jumping up and down, elated as one of my teammates had a long run with the football. Being overweight, I clumsily tripped and fell, fracturing my left wrist. When I got home, my mother took me up the street to see Dr. E. He put a cast on my left wrist, which I carried for about 6 weeks.

When I was 13, I tried out for the Babe Ruth League and was pleased I made it. Each of the teams had uniforms sponsored by local businesses. Our games were all held at a baseball field near Southern Connecticut State

University. I was a pitcher and right-fielder on my team. I had just a fair fastball and an inconsistent curveball. I also didn't hit particularly well but did manage to get a few singles. Those early years enjoying playground sports would set the stage for me to enjoy a lifetime of sports watching following my favorite New York professional teams: the New York Yankees, the New York Football Giants, the New York Knicks, and the New York Rangers. Those were mostly the only teams we could get to see on TV, especially in the early years of the 1950s-1960s before cable television.

Occasionally, I would also watch the New York Giants and Brooklyn Dodgers baseball teams on TV, but I was not as interested in those teams as I was in the Yankees. I was a big fan of Mickey Mantle and thought he was one of the all-time greats. And he was. But after I grew to adulthood, I realized that Willie Mays may well have been the greatest all-around baseball player I ever saw. As a kid, I had a collection of many baseball and football cards. If I had kept them, I would have made some money because many years later, those cards would have become valuable collectors' items if my mother hadn't thrown them out while cleaning my bedroom when I went away to college. But in all fairness to her, she had asked me in a telephone conversation what I wanted her to do with them, and in a weak moment, I mistakenly told her to throw them away.

I remember in the 1950s, my uncle "Brud," my Aunt Irene's husband, took me to see the New York Giants play a Sunday doubleheader against the Chicago Cubs at the old Polo Grounds in upper Manhattan, not too far away from the original Yankee Stadium in the Bronx. We saw the entire first game and left in the third inning of the second game. I also remember seeing the Brooklyn Dodgers play a game at Ebbets Field in the Flatbush section of Brooklyn. I had gone with a group of children from our synagogue in New Haven, and we had seats in the centerfield bleachers right behind Duke Snider. I also remember my father taking me and Mickey L., my Aunt Harriet's brother-in-law, to a night game at the old Yankee Stadium against the Boston Red Sox, with Joe DiMaggio in centerfield for the Yankees and his brother, Dom DiMaggio, in centerfield for the Red Sox, with Ted Williams next to him in rightfield. I recall we sat in a lower-level box down the left-field line.

I had never been to a night game, and I felt there was something magical about being at that game, under the bright lights and with so many star players on both sides, that made it the most exciting baseball game I had ever attended. Some years later, I must have pestered my father to take me to a World Series game during the afternoon, and we sat on the very top deck, which I suppose was the best ticket he could get on relatively short notice. But I cannot now even remember who the Yankees' opponent was. Sitting way up there is not memorable to me because we could have seen the game much better on our own TV.

I have always loved sports, even though I was not that good at playing them in school because I was somewhat overweight and slow. In fact, when I first got to Hopkins in the eighth grade, one of my classmates nicknamed me "Stubby Stu," and it stuck with me through all my years there. I really liked to eat back then. But today, I am about 30 lbs. lighter than in high school because I am now more disciplined in what I eat and how much I eat, and I exercise regularly.

Four or five years ago, I finally gave up watching major league baseball and the Yankees because of what I perceive to be their lack of good management. I also lost my desire to watch NBA games because the Knicks haven't won anything in over fifty years. But I still enjoy watching NFL football, SEC college football, and golf even more than I did as a young man. Unfortunately, I still cannot play golf nearly as well as I would like. But I keep trying. And when I do manage to hit a good shot, I just stare in amazement at the ball that I hit so well. I think much of my problem is just a matter of maintaining my concentration to stay down with the shot throughout the entire swing and not try to hit the ball too hard.

When I was still a little boy, my father and his friend, Harry W., father of my good friend, Michael W., both purchased new cottages next to each other a few short blocks from the beach in the Woodmont section of Milford, CT. I must have been about 8 years old when we first went there for our summers. Our cottage had a white, wood-sided frame with a small kitchen, three small bedrooms that were separated only by partitions that did not go to the ceiling, a small living room, and a nice-sized screened front porch. We also had a built-in summer grill on the rear right side of our house facing the street.

Our house was the last of four modest adjacent cottages on the front-end portion of the street, the top of which we kids had regarded at the time as a hill, but in truth is merely just a slight downgrade, which then continues in a reverse "L" shape with many more houses continuing on towards the beach. We could easily walk to the beach in 10 minutes, usually in a group of two or three of us, with or without our mothers. To the right side of our house, facing the street, there was a large plot of undeveloped grassland, bushes, and trees. Over time, my friends and I created a simple path we used as a shortcut to access the main road that continued to other bigger beaches further down, plus a restaurant named "Sloppy Joe's." The bushes that flanked one side of the path had blackberries that we'd pick to eat on the way to the main road. Such simple things in life that made growing up there so much fun.

I remember one of the first summers I was there, all the kids living in the neighborhood, numbering about 14 of us, got together and decided to put on a play for the parents, charging .25 cents per ticket, with the proceeds going to the Fresh Air Fund. I recall it was a lot of fun practicing our speaking and singing roles, although I really cannot remember what I did. But I think we performed well for a group of child novices. A few of my friends and I used to play wiffleball almost daily in the street. When we were not playing wiffleball, we would go to "the rocks," a stack of big rocks next to the beach down the street from us, to try to fish or look for crabs.

As the years went by, I went to summer overnight camp at Camp Laurelwood in North Madison, CT, and lived in a cabin with 6 other boys, who were either friends of mine or who were acquaintances I had known before, plus our counselor. The Camp was divided into two separate plots of land, with the girls' cabins on one side and the boys' cabins on the other side. The cabins did not have their own toilet facilities, so we had to go outside to a rather spartan, common bathhouse facility we called "the outhouse" to brush our teeth, wash our faces, take showers, and use the toilet. Each of us had a big, black, rectangular trunk filled with our clothing sitting at the foot of our single bunk beds. I think the first time, I went to camp for one month at age 10, and then a few consecutive years later, I went to camp for two months.

The Camp was fun, constantly going to different activities, like softball, basketball, arts & crafts, swimming in the lake, going to the mess hall for lunch and punch, then buying candy at the little outdoor canteen, and taking a short rest in the early afternoon. Sometimes, a few of the counselors would take groups of their campers out into the woods in the afternoon to learn how to build lean-tos out of pieces of wood to provide some shelter in case we ever went camping out. At night, we might often sit around a campfire singing songs that everyone knew or go to a large, planned group activity in the recreation hall. One night, a hypnotist came there. Wouldn't you know it, my friend Michael W. volunteered? And he was hypnotized for what seemed like 20 minutes, doing whatever the hypnotist asked of him. Then, just as fast as the snap of a finger, Michael W. was taken out of the spell. In one of the years I was at camp, I won the honor of male "Camper of the Year." To this day, I still don't know how I managed to do that.

Now that I was 14 years old, my camp days were over, and I really started to be interested in girls. I would see them at the beach in their bikinis, and I would start to feel a bit of tingling inside of me. During the Christmas vacation of 1956, I remember our entire family of five took an airplane from New Haven to Baltimore and then onto Miami and stayed with Grandma Gussie at her little, old bungalow. But we had daily pool privileges at the Sans Souci Hotel in Miami Beach. It had a very big pool, where I met a pretty girl from Toronto, Canada, who was staying at the hotel with her parents.

We did nothing but talk, swim in the pool together, walk on the beach, and look at each other all week. And maybe we even kissed. I truly don't remember. But what I do remember is I began to feel things going on in my body that I had never felt before. Of course, after we flew home, I never saw or heard from that pretty girl again. But she has always been in my heart as the first girl I really looked at with some degree of affection.

One day that summer, I went with friends to one of the bigger beaches further down from where we lived in Woodmont, where we went swimming. I really don't remember who the girl was or what her name was. But I must have met her on the edge of the water and struck up a good conversation. She then jumped in the water, and I jumped in after her. Before I knew it, we were not only swimming together but also holding onto each other. At one point, I could no longer stop myself from putting my hand down between her legs and begin to rub my fingers onto and into her. It lasted for only a few seconds, but she didn't stop me and continued to keep her arms draped over my shoulders. That was my first sexual encounter of any kind at age 14.

I don't remember ever seeing that girl again on subsequent visits to that beach, but you bet I surely kept looking for her during the rest of that summer.

I frankly don't remember any further sexual encounters again until I obtained my driver's license at sixteen in 1958. By then, I was allowed to drive my mother's 1954 two-door, two-tone Pontiac with a stick shift. At a local dance or party, I met a well-built, 15-year-old girl named Dona. She and I would go on to have what became my first sexual relationship. I would pick her up at her house like a gentleman, say hello to her parents, and then take her to the movies or dinner at a local restaurant. On the way home, I would park the car down the darkened street from where she lived, and we would make out and do some serious petting for about an hour. Frankly, I don't remember exactly where or when I first had sex with her, but they were glorious feelings for a boy like me who many times never felt loved enough by my parents. As the relationship progressed into my senior year at Hopkins, I kept wanting more. And she obliged. But my college days were now just around the corner, and our relationship began to flicker away that summer. I did, however, have other love interests, including another good-looking girl with the initials P.M. She was also well-put together and sweet-looking. She and I also enjoyed kissing and having sex. Those days in the 1950s, with all the great rock and roll music, pretty girls, and teenage sex, were a very special time, don't you think?

But coming back down to earth, in September, I went away to Colby College in Waterville, Maine, which at the time didn't seem to have too many good-looking young women. They were all surely very smart, but most were not that attractive to me. In fact, I don't ever remember having sex in the four years I was there. I may have been one of the youngest, if not the youngest, young men in my class. Having entered college at age 17, I was nearly two years younger than many of my freshmen classmates who had post-high school educations before entering college. So, my relative social immaturity may have also played a part in my failure to score with women.

Beginning in my sophomore year, I did make out with a few women at some darkened fraternity parties, with all the free-flowing beer and loud music. But I don't remember that I ever did anything more. Maybe my roommates from college could refresh my recollection. I mostly enjoyed Colby, but I must confess the severe cold weather was not to my liking. If I had to live life all over again, I think I would have preferred going to college in a more moderate climate, like, say, William & Mary College in Virginia or the like. I have previously made known here my displeasure with a certain college inorganic chemistry professor in 1960-61, whose aim apparently was not to really teach but to flunk out as many students as he could. Maybe Colby College can someday find it in its heart to apologize to me and to others for their misguided faith in such a clod? I surely knew I wasn't that stupid when I retook the chemistry class in summer school with much better success.

In May of my senior year at Colby, following a precedent set by previous members of our fraternity, a fraternity brother named Camilo M., and I rented a cabin beside a big, picturesque lake in Oakland, ME, for the purpose of being able to have solitude while studying for our required Comprehensive exams in our major field. After a long Maine winter, students on campus usually went outside in May, enjoying the spring weather and making noise, which was not at all conducive to our studying. My major was history, and there were many books to brush up on in preparation for the exams. With the peace and quiet of the lake area, we were both assured of having the proper environment to study. I'm sure we also had time to get out on the beautiful expanse of the lake in a rowboat. But we didn't abuse our quiet time, and both of us studied long and hard, and fortunately passed our Comp exams. We graduated on a beautiful day in early June 1963 at an outdoor graduation in front of the Colby College library. My parents, sisters, Aunt Harriet, and cousin Jon were all in attendance. They had made the nearly six-hour trip to Waterville, ME, with my parents and sisters to see me graduate, and I was most grateful to both of them for being there.

After college, I went to study law at Suffolk University Law School in Boston. Certainly, I had no time to seek out women. All I did was study, study & study. I think our original class size was about 125, with mostly all men except for four women, one of whom was apparently a nymphomaniac. Believe it or not, I only found this out because she herself told me so. Unbeknownst to any of us students, she told me in confidence she had been "giving head" to the Torts professor. Obviously, I was jealous and wanted some of that, too. So, I said to her in class one day, "Why not me? I am younger and better-looking than him." On one or two occasions, we would meet to study at the college law school library, which was in a relatively small portion of the regular college library, and then leave to meet in one of our cars. Of course, I have never mentioned my dalliances to her to anyone until now. She likely graduated near the top of our class because she was smart, not because she was sexually crazed. I hope she had a good, happy life. And I still think of her occasionally.

In my second year in law school, the class size was substantially smaller. Several men had flunked out, but none of the four women. So, maybe there were half as many students left. I found the second year to be even more challenging than the first year, with courses in Taxation, Property Law, Trusts, and Sales under the Uniform Commercial Code (UCC) and then Secured Transactions under the (UCC), and a few other courses.

Professor Callahan, who taught those two UCC courses and the UCC course in Bank Deposits and Collections, was my favorite law professor at Suffolk Law because he largely used the Socratic method of asking us questions to get us to think about the correct answers rather than just merely dictating information to us.

Again, I had little time to look for women with all the studying I did. And with many thousands of beautiful coeds at Boston University and other colleges in Boston, it was sometimes difficult not to think about doing something other than studying. I do remember going out once with a young woman from Boston University. I don't remember where we had met. She was a beautiful brunette, and I remember I visited her once during Christmas vacation at her home in Hewlett Harbor, Long Island, which was a long drive from New Haven, CT. Unfortunately, I had no additional time to wine and dine with her after that. But, in 1964, perhaps she wasn't too impressed with my second-hand 1957 VW Beetle. I'm very sure she married someone rich. I hope she's had a good, happy life, too.

I had a special relationship that recently came to mind when I began to think about writing this book. One morning, maybe near the start of the second semester of my second year at the law school, I happened to start talking one day to two nice, attractive African-American women who were just standing outside in front of the law school building. I think maybe one of them may have worked nearby, but I never asked them why they were there. They were very pleasant and easy to talk to about almost anything and everything. A few days later, they showed up again. I asked them if they wanted to get coffee down the street. We did so. And one of them seemed interested in me.

I will always remember her because we had a very different kind of relationship for a few months. It wasn't sexual, but it was also more than just platonic. We started seeing each other after school, in my car, in the dark, talking, kissing, and hugging. I really don't think there was any sex involved, except for maybe some minor petting. But she was there for me in a time of need, filling a vacancy in my life with her affection and kindness. I think her name was "Gail," and she lived in Roxbury, MA, which was virtually all black at the time. Maybe still is. She invited me to visit her at her house and have Sunday dinner with her and her parents. And I did so. They were such nice people. We ate and talked on and on about nothing special, but it was fascinating for me to be there with such friendly, courteous people, the kind most White Bigots in our country will never see because they don't even wish to look. After that, I began studying for final exams, but I lost contact with Gail. I never saw her again, and I regret it very much because she was such a good friend of mine at the time. I hope she has had a good, happy life, too.

As previously noted, I spent the summer of 1965 in Washington, D.C., which I still think may be one of the hottest places anywhere to live during the summer. If there weren't a pool to go to, I would stay indoors on the weekends at the apartment near Dupont Circle that I shared with a few other young men. I do remember that at least once, I had met a woman somewhere in the halls of Congress who invited me to a pool at her apartment complex on another side of town. I don't remember her name, but I do remember visiting her and then stripping off our wet bathing suits to engage in some sex. I must have done more than that during the entire summer I spent in Washington, but I simply don't remember the experiences because time has warped my memory.

I have already recited what transpired at the beginning of my third year at law school in Boston when I met my first wife, Irva. She was and still is a friend of mine. I have nothing negative to say about her. At ages 21 and 24, we were simply too young to get married, not knowing enough about our own selves and what we wanted out of life. We had relatively few quarrels, but they always seemed to revolve around her continuing reliance on her mother's opinions, rather than on mine, on several issues. Irva missed her mother and her entire tight family unit, who were all up in New York State, and she wanted to go see them as much as she could. I never blamed her for that, but I needed to spend more time at home to rest and recover from the work I did all week. I felt blessed to have had a beautiful girl, Geri, and then a handsome boy, Brad, three years younger, come into our lives.

Unlike my daughter, Geri, who was born in New Haven, Brad was born in Lawrence Hospital in Bronxville, NY. At birth, Brad had little hair, which was maybe an omen of things to come because he became mostly bald by 30. Like my daughter and me, he was also born in February, so the weather was a bit frosty when he was born. I remember walking tentatively on ice in the hospital parking lot, headed for my parked car, when suddenly my feet flew out in front of me, and I landed flat on my back face-up, looking at the sky, thinking to myself, "Hi God, thanks for the healthy boy."

But after moving back to Connecticut, maybe five years into our marriage, no matter what I tried to do, I could not seem to make either my wife or myself happy. In 1971, I decided to run for First Selectman in Orange, Connecticut. I ran as a Democrat in a town that previously never in its entire history had anyone but a Republican leader. I was a political novice who had never spent any previous time doing any public speaking.

Initially, I was hesitant to speak without looking at my notes, but gradually, I got more confidence in speaking to my audience about the issues that seemed to matter to most residents of the town. It was simply a case of having confidence in myself that allowed me to make a contest out of what everyone had predicted would be a complete trouncing. The man I opposed was not a bad guy, but he was an older, stilted Republican who refused to open his mind to seeking other reasonable solutions to town problems. I didn't realize that most of the leaders in my own Democratic Party were secretly rooting for the re-election of the First Selectman for their own selfish financial interests. I lost the election, but I learned how to speak in public. It just takes practice.

After that, I embarked on a home renewal project to turn our older single-story ranch home into a more contemporary place to live. I brought in an architect acquaintance of mine who drew up the plans that improved the more modern feeling I wanted for our home. Irva was fine with the renovations, which, at the time, seemed expensive, totaling around $20,000. But even with these changes in my life, I was not truly happy, and neither was Irva. We could not seem to give each other what we needed to live a good, meaningful life together. I realized that I could not let my children's future wellness be undermined by my unhappiness. So, I decided separation and/or divorce might be the best course of action.

We went to a few sessions of marriage counseling with a noted psychologist at Yale. But Irva did not wish to take accountability for any of the shortcomings in our marriage. I then set a date at the end of October 1975 to leave the house and let Irva begin the divorce process. My immediate plan was to take up residence for several months at the New Haven Motor Inn, which was owned by my father and my uncle Bernie. I know my children were very upset at this development, but again, I thought it was in their best interests for them to live in a home without so much discord. Irva and I had made a mistake getting married at our young ages, and I was prepared to try to rectify all our lives as much as possible.

My Daughter Geri went to the Monroe, NY, public schools and attended Rockland Community College before transferring to the State University at New Paltz, where she majored in art. She was a somewhat good artist and could have been very good if she had stayed with it. Instead, she met a co-worker named Kevin F. from Washingtonville, NY, who was then working as a salesperson in the same Cole Haan shoe store at the Woodbury Commons in Central Valley, NY. They dated for some time and then were married on May 26, 1996.

A few years later, Geri and Kevin moved to Rhode Island, where Kevin was accepted to law school at Roger Williams School of Law in Bristol, Rhode Island. After his graduation three years later, Kevin was hired by a lawyer in a town not far from Monroe. Later, when his boss retired from the practice, Kevin became the senior partner in that same law firm with two additional attorneys and a paralegal now working for him. On January 26, 2003, Geri gave birth to a son named Jack, who is currently a junior in the engineering program at the University of Buffalo. On August 16, 2005, Geri bore a second son named Matthew, who is now a freshman also in the engineering program at the University of Buffalo. For most of the years, Jack and Matthew grew up, through grade school, middle school, and high school, Geri was a full- or part-time stay-at-home mom for her two sons. Three years ago, Geri was hired by the Monroe, NY, school system to work full-time in a local grammar school, assisting nurses attending to children with COVID, the flu, colds, and other ailments. She is perfect for the job and enjoys the close interactions with the little school children.

My Son Brad also attended the Monroe, NY public schools, then went to college at the University of Connecticut in Storrs, CT. Upon graduating in June 1992 with a B.S. degree in Biology, Brad went to The New England College of Optometry in Boston, MA, where he earned a Doctor of Optometry (OD) degree. Brad then moved back to Monroe, married his long-time girlfriend, Jackie, on September 1, 1996, and went to work for her father at his Monroe Family Eyecare, a leading optometrist in that area. Brad has now long been a partner there with three other optometrists. Brad and his wife, Jackie, have two sons, Jordan, a graduate of the University of Wisconsin, and Ethan, a junior at the University of Wisconsin, and a daughter, Madison, a senior at Monroe-Woodbury High School, who is now filing applications to several colleges.

Before I left home at the end of October 1975, I just happened to call a friend of mine from Orange, Michael C., and tell him about my pending separation or divorce. He uttered a quick laugh and then told me he, too, was soon getting a divorce. We and our wives had gone out together for dinner or the movies on a few occasions, so I was surprised he was also in the same position I was in. He told me he was moving to a large apartment complex in Hamden, CT, just outside New Haven. Around that time, I met an interesting woman at a local bar in the Westville section of New Haven. She invited me to meet her the following night at her apartment, and we talked for hours, mostly about what I was going through in my life. She seemed to be a nice friend I could talk to.

I recall my friendship with that woman later developed into a more sexual relationship. And that was apparently not at all expected by her girlfriend, who saw me as her rival. I never realized that the woman I had been with was somewhat of a sexual oddity, at least for me, a bi-sexual who was comfortable having ongoing sex with men as well as women, perhaps at the same time. After a month or two of being in her company with her gay and lesbian friends, who used to mingle of all places in the bar down the street from where I grew up on Chapel Street, she began to become more aloof and stopped calling me. I then learned from another woman who knew her that I had created a problem in her life with her woman friend, so the relationship was ended. I learned a bit about life in the world of LGBTQ in the short time I knew her. I think her name was "Gail," too, but I'm not sure. Anyway, I hope she had a good, happy life, too.

In January 1976, my sister Janet and her then-husband, Stan, invited me to join them on a trip to San Juan, Puerto Rico, for a week in the sun. I think we stayed at a condominium owned by someone Stan knew. And we had pool privileges at a well-known local hotel there. I had fun being away together with them, but at the same time, I thought they should have some time alone without me. One night I ventured off to an area by myself that just happened to be where hookers hung out. I didn't know that at the time. But I remember there were two near each other together; one was white, and the other was black. I didn't find the white woman very attractive, so I chose the better-looking black one. I forget where we went, but it was probably in a room up a flight of stairs from where we were standing outside. And she took care of me very well. It was the only time I've ever been with a hooker. I don't think I ever told my sister how much I appreciated the time we had in San Juan.

Sometime in early 1976, I moved out of the New Haven Motor Inn into a nice one-bedroom apartment in the same apartment complex as my friend, Michael C. It had a nice pool for swimming a little in the hot summer months, which gave me hope I could meet a woman there. I met a few, but my main interest centered on a woman who lived in a smaller garden apartment complex across the street from there. Her name is Marilyn D. She and I hit it off almost immediately. She was smart and had a good sense of humor that I found to my liking. She also had a good body, with ample breasts and good lips. We spent at least one and one-half happy years together. We took an accounting course together, camped out a few times in a tent under the stars, went out to dinners and the movies, cooked dinners together, listened to music high on pot, and perhaps best of all, she was a good sex partner. We also took a vacation together for a week in St. Croix in the Virgin Islands, staying with my parents. A friend of my father had loaned him the use of a terrific condo overlooking the famous Buck Island Reef National Monument on the arid side of the island. We went snorkeling there and saw a great many beautiful fish around the Reef.

If I hadn't just been coming out of a marriage, I might otherwise have chosen her as a mate. I will always have a soft spot in my heart for her, and I hope she has had a good, happy life, too.

Around the beginning of January 1977, I took a business trip, which gave me the opportunity to visit my aunt, uncle, and cousins, Paul and Carol, in a suburb of San Francisco, California. Carol had joined a health club near her called the European Health Spa. I went with her a few times while I was out there and realized that I was then an out-of-shape, middle-aged man who needed to exercise. When I got home, I joined the local European Health Spa in Hamden near me. It began what has now been over forty-seven years of exercising my body, doing weight training, and cardio. In fact, within six months of becoming a gym member, I also began to jog a little each day and progressed to jogging longer distances as time passed in all kinds of weather. Physical exercise, staying toned and healthy, has surely been the best thing I ever did for myself, improving both my mind and my body.

That Spring, I also became interested in photography, and I bought my first good camera, a Canon F-1, plus a few lenses for both distance and closeness. I began taking photos of birds and flowers, a lot of flowers. I loved getting up close to the center of the flower petals to go inside to see what my naked eye could not see. I enjoyed being an amateur photographer using that camera because it did not have a predetermined set of f/stops, which meant I could experiment a little with what I wished to use. I had a few good years of real enjoyment with that camera.

In February 1977, my friend Michael C. and I decided to go on a vacation to Club Med in Martinique in the French Caribbean. Even before we left the JFK Airport on a charter flight from New York, Michael had already spotted a woman in the passenger terminal he wanted to meet. He started up a conversation there, and he ended up being with her for the entire seven days we were at Club Med. I was fine being alone, making new friends, eating good food, lying on the beach with women, and viewing the best sunset I have ever seen, together with a piped-in classical musical to honor the occasion. It is still the only sunset into the water I ever saw that was totally without any obstruction. We both enjoyed our time there but in very different ways.

My divorce became final in March 1977, and I began thinking about perhaps moving closer to my workplace in Stamford, CT, because Hamden is at least an hour away by car. My urge to move closer was greatly heightened by the massive blizzard Connecticut and the northeast suffered between February 5-7, 1978. The trip from Stamford to Hamden, normally about an hour, that day took me about three hours to get home. The snow was so high it covered most cars in the parking lots of the apartment complex I lived in, as well as the parking lots of the large shopping centers right below that. In fact, I could not even get my car into the lot of the apartment building I lived in, so I left it in the first vacant area I could find in the parking lot of the nearby shopping center. I recall Governor Ella Grasso, at the time, ordered the Connecticut highways closed to traffic for at least the next day or two, including the Merritt Parkway that I used to travel on.

In June 1978, my now former wife, Irva, moved with our two children from their rental in New Haven to live in an apartment in her hometown of Monroe, NY, in Orange County, NY, about one hour north of Manhattan. Of course, I was very sorry to see my children leave Connecticut, but I felt in my heart it was in their best interests for their schooling and for the family support they would receive from Irva's mother, father, sister, aunts and uncles, and cousins all living there. And the schools at that time were much better for them there than in New Haven.

My Daughter Geri went to the Monroe, NY, public schools and attended Rockland Community College before transferring to the State University at New Paltz, where she majored in art. She was a somewhat good artist and could have been even better if she had stayed with it. Instead, she met a co-worker named Kevin F. from Washingtonville, NY, who was then working in the same Cole Haan shoe store at the Woodbury Commons in Central Valley, NY. They dated for some time and then were married on May 26, 1996. Then, with Geri, Kevin went to law school for three years at Roger Williams School of Law in Bristol, Rhode Island. After graduation, Kevin was hired by a lawyer in a town not far from Monroe, who later retired from the practice.

Kevin became the senior partner in that same law firm, with two additional attorneys and a paralegal now working for him. On January 26, 2003, Geri gave birth to a son named Jack, who is currently a junior in the engineering program at the University of Buffalo. On August 16, 2005, Geri bore a second son named Matthew, who is now a freshman in the engineering program at the University of Buffalo. For most of the years Jack and his younger brother, Matthew, grew up, Geri was mostly a full- or part-time stay-at-home mom for her two sons. A few years ago, Geri was hired by the Monroe, NY school system to work full-time in a local grammar school, assisting nurses who were attending to children with COVID, the flu, colds, and other ailments. She is perfect for the job and enjoys the close interactions with the little school children.

My Son Brad also attended the Monroe, NY public schools, then went to college at the University of Connecticut in Storrs, CT. Upon graduation in June 1992 with a B.S. degree in Biology, Brad went to The New England College of Optometry in Boston, MA, where he earned a Doctor of Optometry (OD) degree. Brad then moved back to Monroe, married his long-time girlfriend, Jackie, on September 1, 1996, and went to work for her father at his Monroe Family Eyecare, a leading optometrist in that area. Brad has long been a partner there with three other optometrists. Brad and his wife, Jackie, have two sons, Jordan, now a graduate of the University of Wisconsin; Ethan, a junior at the University of Wisconsin; and a daughter, Madison, a senior at the Monroe-Woodbury High School, who is now filing applications to several colleges.

All in all, in retrospect, I think my decision to part ways with Geri and Brad's mother in March 1977 turned out well for them because they grew up in a happy home without a lot of hurtful discord, and they became role models for other children of divorced parents. It would also have turned out well for Irva, too, if her second husband, Richard, had not died so young from pancreatic cancer many years ago. He was a good and decent man who left behind a daughter, Maitreya, who is now grown and lives in California. I am grateful to him for the paternal guidance he provided to Geri and Brad while they were growing up.

In the summer of 1978, I began to make the first of my few travels to Westport, CT, to look for a house to purchase. I did not have much money. My portion of the proceeds from the sale of our home in Orange left me with a net amount of only about $15,000. Of that, I used $8,500 as a down payment on an appealing $85,000 little, two-bedroom ranch up a long driveway high upon a hill overlooking the main road into the center of Westport, a few minutes away from an entrance to and exit from, the Merritt Parkway. I wish I had had more money to buy a home near the water of Long Island Sound at that time because housing prices absolutely exploded in the nearly twenty-years I owned the house in that sweet town. I was always very content living up on the hill, mainly because it was very shady with many, many trees both in front and back of the house, making it almost hidden from the traffic below, heading into and out of the town.

The first thing I did after I moved into the house in September 1978 was to spend a little money on renovation, perhaps $3,000 or so, to get rid of the large permanent window in the living room and substitute sliding glass doors instead. I also had a good-sized wooden deck built right next to the house. The only other major investment I added was a large attic fan to take out warm air and leave the house cooler.

During many of the years I lived in Westport, I went to the gym almost as an afterthought because my first love was running in the early morning hours before work every day. And I did it for at least ten years. I loved the exhilarating feeling running gave me, with a runner's high from endorphins kicking in. I would run early every morning, around 5:30 a.m., from my house on Fragrant Pines Court down behind Main Street, go across Route 1 to Saugatuck Avenue, then up Bridge Street to Compo Road North, across Route 1 and back home, a total distance of about 5.5 miles. In addition, I entered several 10k races in Westport, Stamford, and other nearby towns. The longest race I ever entered was the New Haven Road Race on Labor Day. It was a 20k that required many months of conditioning and race preparation. I finished that race within my set goal of less than four hours. But it took a lot out of me.

For the first year that I lived in Westport, I did not have much of a social life while still getting acclimated to my new surroundings. Across the street from my house, there was a little strip plaza with a convenience store, a dry cleaner, and an auto service garage. Across a narrow street from that was a restaurant with a bar that never had much attraction for me. So, I mostly stayed in reading good books. I read the works of some great authors. Among my all-time favorite books were the two great historical novels about World War II by Herman Wouk, entitled "The Winds of War" and "War and Remembrance," in which the author used fictional characters set in this period of history to convey the social and military conditions of that time with realistic detail including the names of real-world leaders and personages.

Following those books, I also very much enjoyed many of the fictional novels written by Richard North Patterson, which interjected constitutional law issues of note that are still meaningful today. Then, over time, I began to venture out on weekends to visit the local health food and vitamin store, a terrific cheese shop, a big clothing store, and other fine offerings in this little town. Its Main Street was then a street filled with many small, family-owned businesses on both sides of the street, which included a hardware store, a camera shop, a pink bookstore, a small take-out pizza restaurant, some clothing shops, jewelry stores, and miscellaneous other retail shops. Years later, these same stores would be gobbled up by the retail giants that could pay much higher rents for them, especially with sufficient, convenient additional parking in the backs of the stores along the Saugatuck River. I took to the town like a kid in a candy shop, taking in as much of it as I could. I then began to look for nightspots and found a good one on Route 1 and another across from the Westport Railroad Station. They just felt right for me. And I began to meet both men and women who appealed to me as friends.

Unfortunately, the next summer, my little secluded house left me open to a few burglaries of my possessions, namely my prized camera, the Canon F-1, and my 24" television. I had unwittingly enabled the burglaries by opening a window to my bedroom in the rear of the house to allow in fresh air but failed to properly secure it by locking it in place. I thought it was just a one-and-done experience, but the very next summer, I was burglarized again. This time, the bandits stole my school ring and some other jewelry of no particular significance because I really had nothing of real value. The police who arrived following each of the burglaries thought they were the work of some young punks who were out to get money to buy drugs.

Now, I finally took the action of hiring a handyman to put locks in the windows, which, of course, I should have done before.

I think the first friends I met in Westport were Steve D. and Arnie S. They were both manufacturers' sales reps; one sold for a national men's clothing company, and the other sold an entire line of equipment mostly to regional food supermarket chains. They were both intelligent men around my age but appeared to be more street-smart than me, the straight-arrow corporate tax attorney. They often traveled for business and likely earned much more money than me. Soon after, a successful New York businessman named Steve R. joined the three of us to make up a rather unique quartet. We all went out frequently to eat and drink together, especially on weekend nights. We also went to parties and had great fun over the years hanging out on the weekends at the local Compo Beach, looking at and talking to the women. I also played golf often with Steve D. at the Longshore Golf Course. Though neither of us was very good at golf, we surely had great fun playing golf together over the years.

One summer, I remember all of us rented a house for a week on Martha's Vineyard together with our girlfriends. Arnie and I brought our bikes and, in the mornings, rode all over the island, from Vineyard Haven to Oak Bluffs to

Edgartown, many miles of good bike riding. Those are the memories I still carry with me today. It would be difficult ever to replicate again what the four of us had together during those many years. I surely miss those days. I think in 1980, I grew a beard for just about one year. When I see the photo of me with my beard, it brings back good memories of the several years I would often visit my friend who owned the Camera Shop on Main Street in Westport to develop my photos. She was a sweet woman.

The first woman I dated in Westport was a good-looking brunette named Barbara T, whom I had met at a local bar. At the time, she was either divorced or separated and the mother of twin girls who were still in high school in Wilton, CT. She had much of what I had greatly lacked in my marriage: an affectionate woman who really appreciated me. We even went away together to Club Med in Guadeloupe in the French Caribbean. She was a very good athlete who could windsurf/sailboard far better than anyone else at the Club Med, and especially clumsy me. I could not even stand up on the board without falling. Barbara was so good at it; in just a matter of just a few seconds, she was way out in the deep water near big rocks, and she needed to be helped back into the local area. Otherwise, she might have gone to another island. But Barbara was the victim of my wanderlust, and not because she wasn't a suitable woman for me. After nearly two years together, I found another woman who caught my fancy. I have remained in contact with Barbara's twin daughters on Facebook, and I have reached out to Barbara a few times in the hope she has had a good, happy life, too.

The next woman I was with was also named Barbara but with an H. She was still married when I met her, and not even separated, and had two sons. I still regret it, but it wasn't my fault because she was seeking to get out of a bad marriage. Barbara was the first true artist in my life. She painted in oils, and for the most part, her work was interesting. Art is usually subjective anyway, viewed from the eyes of the beholder. Barbara and I had a very good sexual relationship for well over a year. But then, gaps in our mutual interests began to set in, heightened by our surreptitious meetings and my desire to rid myself of the guilty feelings of my contribution to breaking up a marriage. The end of the relationship came when she gave me an ultimatum not to go to Europe with Marjorie. But I did anyway.

Marjorie was an interesting woman who was not very physically appealing to me, but her mind surely was. She was extremely smart and very well-educated. She and I were just good friends, but she would have hoped for much more. Early in the summer of 1985, she offered to take me to Europe for two weeks, which she fully paid for.

At the time, I was still seeing Barbara H., but I regarded Marjorie's invitation as the way to finally rid myself of the unfortunate situation I had gotten myself into and instead visit several European countries. It was a chance of a lifetime, and I simply could not pass it up. So off we went. I didn't realize before we went that Marjorie was fluent in both German as well as Swiss German, so everywhere we went, language was absolutely no problem. We went to many cities in Europe that I could only dream about. Upon arriving in Frankfurt, we traveled by car through Germany on the Autobahn, stopping in Cologne to see the magnificent Cathedral there, and then went on to Munich. Next, we went to Basel. Then, I went to Zurich and saw some of the sights in that beautiful city, and then to Bern, the capital of Switzerland. We even went to little Liechtenstein, which is a tiny little country. We then drove through the Swiss Alps, staying overnight in a beautiful hotel in the upscale resort town of Gstaad.

One of my favorite stops was Salzburg, Austria, for a few reasons. One reason was we were fortunate to be able to go up an outdoor elevator to a historical Medieval Castle up on a hill overlooking Salzburg, where a classical music summer concert was held inside an old knights' room, with all the armor and shields from days of yore displayed on the walls. We were privileged to listen to four members of the Berlin Symphony Orchestra play in that outstanding venue. After the concert, we had reservations for dinner at a very special restaurant where many men and women from Salzburg's high society were dressed up in their tuxedos and formal gowns. It was an amazing evening. The other reason for being there was the town next to Salzburg, called "Golling," which may well have been where my grandfather Benjamin's family originally came from.

I was in awe of this clean, little town where a funeral was being held that very day, with people marching in the street behind a rolling, horse-drawn cart carrying the body of some leading member of the community who was being laid to rest. After Salzburg, I drove at least eight hours south by car through many tunnels in Italy to Monaco and then to the beaches of Cannes and Saint-Tropez. They were all amazing to visit. And my friend Marjorie made this great trip possible. Like many people I have met along my life's journey, I lost contact with Marjorie. I hope she has had a good, happy life, too, because she was such a kind person to me.

Several months after that trip, maybe towards the end of 1986, I met a perky woman whose birthday happened to be on the same date as mine. Her name is Bonnie, and we had a few great years together. She had just recently been divorced when we first met, and she surely filled a void in my life. She had given birth to two lovely daughters when she was age 19 and/or 20, who largely kept her from ever going to college. But she was, nevertheless, quite street smart and owned her own women's clothing store. She had great taste in clothes, and I think we hit it off right away because she was cheerful and upbeat with a peppy personality. We had many fun times together that I still remember years later. But I must take major fault for the demise of our close relationship due to my own work insecurity at the time.

I was very much uncertain of my future as an attorney, and that's why I moved to Florida to study for and take the Florida Bar Exam. I never blamed her for moving on to find a suitable man to replace me. I think there will always be a special bond between us. And I believe she has had a good, happy life with her husband, Ed.

During the many years I lived in that house, I had many other sex partners. I frankly don't remember most of their names, where they all came from, or when I met them. But I must have been very much addicted to sex because I remember in one week being in my bed with four different women. I say this not with any sense of braggadocio but rather to be factually correct about my life during much of the 1980s in Westport, CT. But I also realized I had nothing else with most of them except sex. There were no lingering ties with good, satisfying personal relationships. Perhaps I was due to change my life with more fulfilling, monogamous relationships. I often think about the balance in one's life, from having periods of plenty to also hitting dry spells.

When I moved to Jupiter, FL, in 1990, I thought about trying to hang onto Bonnie, but it was not to be. I did nothing but work and study for the entire four and-one-half months I was in Florida. Every night from Monday to Friday, after working a full day at the aircraft trading company and then making myself a quick dinner, I would hunker down with one or more cassette tapes on my TV showing presentations of different areas of Florida law and/or federal constitutional law. Because constitutional case law is not static, there were many more new significant constitutional law cases I had to learn about than there were in 1966, when I had previously taken the Connecticut Bar Exam. I remember my daughter, Geri, visited me from New York one weekend in June 1990, and we went to the beach in Jupiter, swam in the pool at the apartment, and went out to dinner a few times. I also remember that after I drove her to the airport in West Palm Beach and dropped her off for her flight back to New York, her flight didn't leave for quite some time as previously scheduled due to thunderstorms in the New York area. I thought the Florida Bar Exam was very difficult because it had so many long, multiple-choice questions, as opposed to all the written essays to questions I had to answer on the Connecticut Bar Exam twenty-four years earlier.

When I learned several weeks later that I had passed the Florida Bar Exam, naturally, I was extremely relieved and elated knowing I did not have to take the exam again, especially at the age of 48, being one of the older exam takers.

By then, I had already returned to Connecticut, where my life was not that pleasant. As previously noted, I did not then have a job, and I could not even live in my own home because I had leased it before I had left for Florida. Whether I should have stayed in Florida in 1990 after I took the Florida Bar Exam is perhaps a question for debate. But I chose to go back to the place I knew best. The owner of the aircraft trading company in Jupiter, who had fired me, was a mean-spirited person who attempted to prevent my receipt of any Florida Unemployment Compensation. But I challenged him and received the relatively small amounts to which I was entitled for the next six months. It was really what I had to live on, together with some of my modest savings at that time. I lived at Maizie's home in Fairfield until early February 1991. She proved to be a true friend who helped me in a time of need. I hope she has had a good, happy life.

After I accepted the tax attorney position offered by the DRS in early 1991, I moved from Fairfield to a condominium complex in Rocky Hill, CT, which was about a half-hour ride with traffic on I-84 into Hartford. The condominium did not seem very old and had two levels, with a kitchen, dining area, and living room on the first floor, as well as two bedrooms and a bathroom upstairs. I furnished it with the purchase of used furniture from an older man in West Hartford who had advertised it for sale and had kept it stored in a garage behind his house. The rent was affordable for me, and I appreciated living there because a fine, narrow, little golf course was also right next to it that I frequented on the weekends. While I lived there, I had a few short flings with some women whose names no longer come to mind. Although I made some friends during the six years I lived there, I never felt as connected as I had been in Westport, CT, at the other end of the State.

By then, my sister Janet had been divorced from her husband Stan, who I had personally liked, and thought was a good guy. But their marriage had long ended before that, and Janet still lived in her home with her two daughters in Orange, CT.

Later, In 1991, Janet introduced to our family an upbeat, cheerful, smiley friend of hers, a man with red-orange hair named Dennis D. He was a teacher in the same school system in Oxford, CT, where Janet was a speech therapist for children needing help with their speaking. Dennis was a rare, special, one-of-a-kind man. He was not only an extremely good-natured individual but also someone you took an instant liking to because you could tell he was for real, not at all insincere like some other men I had met. Almost one year after I had returned from Florida, in the late Spring-early summer of 1991, I decided to repaint the inside of my house before the next tenant moved in. And Dennis was right there with me, helping me paint my house while my friends in Westport were off doing something else.

Dennis also trusted me very much. When he asked me where I'd suggest he should put his money into real estate, I advised him to find a location near Long Island Sound. A few days later, Dennis called me back and told me he had put a deposit on a house in Milford, CT, right in front of a beach. It was an attractive, good-sized, multi-level house with a wrap-around deck overlooking the beach and Long Island Sound.

I congratulated Dennis and Janet on selecting their new home together. But Dennis was never the type of person to boast about his purchase and was just so happy and pleased that he had found a good home for them. They were not yet even engaged, but no one cared, including my parents, who also liked Dennis very much. In the summer of 1992, there was a major hurricane named "Andrew" that first hit Florida and then went all the way up the East Coast to Connecticut and created a great deal of property damage along the coastline, with severe flooding that badly wrecked almost the entire lower level of their home in Milford. I was living in Rocky Hill, CT, which is at least an hour's drive from Milford.

I offered to help Dennis clean up the water-damaged flooring and walls on that lower level. We spent most of one day cleaning out the debris from the ravaged interior. Following that day, Dennis and Janet were able to secure adequate funding from their insurance carrier to provide a satisfactory refurbishment of that lower level. Then, in the first quarter of 1993, Janet and Dennis were finally married at their home in front of family and friends, and it was a joyous occasion for all.

Dennis and Janet celebrated his 50th birthday on September 30, 1993, at a nearby restaurant. Following that evening, Dennis began experiencing pain in his stomach area. Tests were done, and it was determined after a few weeks of more testing that Dennis could possibly have pancreatic cancer. He was admitted to Saint Mary's Hospital in Waterbury for treatment. Dennis had grown up in the Waterbury area, and it seemed to be the hospital he and his family knew best. But after a few months, Dennis was transported to Yale-New Haven Hospital for further treatment of his pancreatic cancer.

I visited Dennis as much as I could at the hospital. I truly loved the man like a brother. Before he got sick, when I visited him at home, he would ask me to go for a ride with him to get a big cup of coffee at his favorite fast-food restaurant. This wasn't in the morning, but rather late in the day or even early at night. In a candid moment during the latter stage of Dennis' illness, he admitted to me that maybe he had too much coffee, which could have adversely affected his pancreas. I asked his doctor one day, when Dennis was out of his room, if too much-caffeinated coffee could have contributed to his cancer, and he said it was very possible. Dennis died in February 1994, less than four and half months after the onset of his illness. A memorial service was held for Dennis in Milford a few days after his death, attended by many of his friends and family members.

I still miss him to this day. He was one of the three best men I have ever known in my life.

One of the new friends I had met at one of the singles groups while I was living in Rocky Hill was a woman named Jen. She lived in a much larger condominium complex in Avon, CT. She and I were just friends and nothing more. I had gone to many singles functions over the years while I was working in Hartford, but I never made a real connection to any woman I cared about. In the middle of December 1996, Jen called me and asked if I was going to the singles group's Christmas dinner.

I said, "Oh, I don't know. It's probably just more of the same ole stuff."

Her response was, "Well, there is a new woman who just moved in here. Do you want to meet her?"

I agreed to go with them in Jen's car to the Christmas dinner on December 20, 1996. We met in a shopping center parking lot in Cromwell, CT, not too far from the entrance to Route 9 that she took to get us to the small town and cozy restaurant in Chester, CT, where the Christmas dinner was being held. I got in the back seat and said hello to Jen's new friend, Jeri. We made small talk on the way there.

Being dark, I didn't really get to see Jeri until we got out of the car. As we were walking toward the front door on some icy patches, she reached out her hand for me to help her get inside. We ended up sitting next to each other at the Christmas dinner. And we both seemed to really enjoy each other's company. I learned that she had just moved to Avon from Memphis, TN, where she had been engaged in marketing senior living communities. Jeri was a brunette with an attractive, thin face, green eyes, and a good figure. She told me she had first attended the University of Pittsburgh, then transferred to George Washington University in Washington, D.C., and then later added advanced degrees in her chosen fields, including a Ph.D., which she received at a college in Florida. We had an enjoyable dinner together. When we left, I asked her if she would be interested in going out sometime. She said, "Yes, of course." But she told me the very next day she was going on a trip with a singles group to Thailand for two weeks. I wished her a great trip and asked her to please call me when she returned, which she did.

At the time I met Jeri, I had been seeing another woman named Arlene, who lived in a town at least twenty miles outside Hartford. She and I had gone out to dinner on a few occasions, and she seemed quite pleasant. After a few weeks of seeing her, she invited me to accompany her to the wedding of her son, who was then a medical student at the University of Vermont. We went there for a weekend near the end of December 1996 that included a day of snowshoeing with her through woods in Burlington, VT. I had never done that, and it was exhilarating. In fact, after she had had enough and stopped, I continued snowshoeing by myself for another hour or so because it was so much fun.

I had never taken to snow skiing, but I will never forget my day snowshoeing in Vermont. I really don't remember the wedding or much of anything else of the weekend with her, but I do recall that when we returned from Vermont, I had some misgivings about continuing our relationship. There was something that just did not feel right. One night, soon after our return, I went to see her, but her little dog would not stop barking at me, which seemed to set the tone for the evening. I do remember not accepting her invitation to stay for the night and deciding instead to drive home after listening to her little barking dog that had gotten me so upset. Unfortunately, I did not know at the time that I would have to drive through a rather big snowstorm that had just started after 10:00 pm while I was on my way home to my condo in Rocky Hill. It was a rather harrowing experience driving at night through the snowstorm, but I got there safe and sound. By the time I arrived, I had already made the decision to pursue Jeri when she returned from her trip.

I thought Jeri was the sort of well-educated, kind woman I was looking for. When she returned from her trip, we dated heavily for four months, and we had some sex. Then, in April 1997, she invited me to move in with her at her condominium for one year on an interim basis.

Frankly, I was very pleased. But then the unforgettable move took place, and I still think about it on occasion. I rented a U-Haul truck not far from my workplace in Hartford. But when I picked it up, there was little or no gasoline in the tank, according to the reading on the dashboard. So, I needed to get gas. In the meantime, my son Brad, who was then still attending the University of Connecticut in Storrs, CT, and my friend, Steve D., was already at my condominium in Rocky Hill, ready to help me move my furniture and put it into the truck. But when I went to the rather small gas station near the U-Haul facility in Hartford, it was located on a corner with very little access room in or out of the station, especially with a big truck. I made the turn with the truck, but I cut it just a bit short and found myself right up against one of the gasoline pumps.

A man came running out of the station yelling, "Stop, stop," which I did.

Then, over the next hour, I had quite a difficult experience trying to maneuver the truck away from the gasoline pump and then be able to purchase enough gasoline to make the trip from Hartford to Rocky Hill, pick up the furniture, and take it to Avon, where Jeri lived. But with the help of the gasoline attendant, I was finally able to extricate myself from that gasoline pump and get out of there. Being that mobile phones were not yet available, I had no way to reach my son and my friend, Steve, who were both waiting outside my condo without any idea what had taken me so long.

I got some very strange looks from them when I finally arrived with the truck at my condo, ready to pick up my furniture. I explained what happened and thanked them both for helping me make the move to Jeri's condominium in Avon. Jeri had purchased her condo before she had permanently left Memphis. It was much larger than the one I had been renting in Rocky Hill. It had a bigger kitchen, a separate dining room, a much larger living room with a view to the golf course in the back, plus a walk-up rear deck. Upstairs, the spare bedroom was used as a computer room, and the master bedroom and bath were both much larger than mine.

Jeri and I were happy together for that year. I would awaken at 4:30 am every other morning to go to the local gym, which opened at 5:00 am. I continued my workouts at the gym like I had begun many years before. I did all the cooking from the very start of our relationship because I had been cooking for myself during the more than twenty- years in which I had been single, from 1976 to 1997. Jeri had made a few initial attempts to cook our meals, but they did not turn out as well as mine. Plus, Jeri didn't have as much time to prepare meals as I did since her job required her to spend longer hours at work. When the year was up, Jeri's ultimatum to me was that I had to either agree to marry her or leave. But I loved her very much for being the sweet, gentle, good-natured, kind woman she is. And so, I agreed to marriage.

Jeri and I then took off for a long weekend to go to Florida to visit her mother, Ruth, to receive her stamp of approval. She was a very attractive, statuesque woman with short gray hair who was living alone in a beautiful, large house in Lantana, FL, that had both the contemporary look and open landscape design I liked. Jeri's father, Richard, had unfortunately passed away several years before of pancreatic cancer. Since I never met this nice-looking man, his photos provided a way for me to see where Jeri got some of the distinguishing features in her face, like her mouth. My parents had already met Jeri on a few occasions. In fact, Jeri really hit it off with my father, who by then was 80 years old. Their birthdays were also two days apart, so they also had that in common. I know my parents appreciated the fact I was not marrying some bimbo but instead an educated woman with a good heart and soul. God knows they waited a long, long time for me to get married again. In fact, there was a twenty-one-year difference between the end of my first marriage in 1977 and the beginning of my second marriage in June 1998.

I remember telling my father at dinner when my divorce from Irva was official that he didn't have to worry about me being on a quick rebound between marriages. But I think he also thought twenty-one years was far too long. Jeri had had two previous, unfortunate, short-term marriages that also didn't end well. The first one crashed because the young man she married decided afterward he didn't want children. The second of her marriages was to someone who apparently drank too much and likely didn't help Jeri much financially.

I planned a rather low-key, informal, jacket-and-tie wedding on a little beach in Stratford, CT, next to a small restaurant overlooking Long Island Sound, where we would have a sit-down dinner following the marriage service. The date was June 28, 1998. The weather was picture-perfect, and the location was ideal and quite accessible for most of the invited guests who were from the southwestern part of the State. It was surely an attractive place for the two of us to be wed in front of our family and friends. I think there may have been fewer than fifty couples at the wedding, which was officiated by my friend, the former President of the Westport Rotary Club, Stan A., an attorney in Westport who I had always admired. He had never met most of the guests, including my father, but you would never have guessed it by the way his cordial relationship with my father developed almost instantaneously like they had been lifelong buddies.

Jeri looked beautiful in the dress she had purchased for the occasion in a little boutique by the side of the road in Woodbury, CT. Her head of hair was on full display in a lovely hairdo that she now tells me I had helped her put together before the wedding. After the short wedding service on the beach, pictures were taken, and then everyone went into the restaurant for a pleasant sit-down dinner, accompanied by a young classical guitarist who played easy-listening music throughout the dinner. It turned out to be a glorious day for us, and everyone had a wonderful time.

Jeri had previously owned a female Shih-Tzu dog, and she was interested in having another female. In the early fall, we saw an ad in the local Hartford paper offering new Shih-Tzu puppies at a house in Thompson, CT. I didn't realize how far it was from Avon. We drove more than an hour through many backroads in Connecticut to get there and found a few cute, pretty puppies to pick from in the backyard.

One was running around and around a tree chasing a Jack Russell Terrier, and another one was just sitting on a chair looking prim and proper at the others playing, taking it all in. We chose the Shih-Tzu chasing the Jack Russell Terrier for its spirited behavior. She was a cute, white dog about 11 lbs. in weight. It was a novel experience for me driving home with a new little dog. I had owned a male West Highland Terrier with Irva, named "Muffin," but that was well over twenty years earlier. We named our dog "Sasha." We soon learned from the veterinarian that Sasha had a heart murmur, but he did not think it would necessarily be a long-term problem.

On most weekends, I used to take Sasha for long walks through the woods and on trails at the Reservoir in West Hartford. Unfortunately, during the week, once I took Sasha for a short walk to do her business in the early morning hours, she spent too many long days in her crate until I arrived home from work around 5:00 pm. And Jeri got home from work between 6:30-7:00 pm. Sasha's spirit as an animal may very well have been adversely affected by the long days she spent in the crate while we were at work, as well as retarding the development of her personality. I always felt guilty going off to the gym before 5:00 am leaving her in her crate. Jeri got up a few hours later but did not have much involvement in either feeding or walking the dog because she was busy getting ready for work.

In the summer of 2001, my mother told me my father had been complaining about pain in the lower jaw on one side of his mouth. He and my mother went to see a dentist, as well as a few doctors in Florida, trying to figure out what was wrong. For the previous ten or so years, they had lived during the winters in their very modest condo apartment in quite a large senior community in Coconut Creek, FL, called "Wynmoor Village," and then would spend the summers up in Milford, CT at my sister Janet's home that overlooked a beach there.

When Jeri and I would drive down from Avon to visit my parents at Janet's home, I remember my father would anxiously wait for us to arrive, standing on a little balcony outside the front door so he could be the first to greet us. Their lives up until then had been very good. Their principal doctor had been in Connecticut, but they also saw local doctors in their Florida town when they were there. Over a period of several years, all of them prescribed blood tests, but for whatever reason, none prescribed for my father the appropriate PSA blood tests for prostate cancer. I was 59 at the time and had already been receiving my regular PSA tests for many years.

At my next birthday, I will be the same age as my father was when he learned from a Florida doctor that he had prostate cancer that had metastasized to other areas of his body, including his lower jaw. Evidently, he soon went downhill fast, and in late July, my mother called me asking me to come to Florida to say my goodbyes. I was very sad and flew down alone. When I arrived at the hospital on July 31, 2001, my father was on a ventilator and in a virtual coma. But I held his hand and squeezed gently while speaking to him, saying that I was now there with him. And he knew I was there because he squeezed my hand in return. It was such a difficult thing for all of us to have to say goodbye to him after so many wonderful years together.

I left the hospital that night, and the next morning, my mother called to tell me my father had passed in the early morning hours of August 1. We then scheduled his Jewish funeral for three days later at the same funeral home in Boca Raton, FL, where my uncle Bernie's funeral had been held nearly seven years earlier. My uncle Bernie had been diagnosed with lung cancer in the early 1990s while he was still living in Boynton Beach, FL, and then he died within a few years later. Jeri took a flight down to Florida a day or two after me to attend the funeral service for my father. Before the service, each member of our family had the opportunity to say his/her final private goodbyes to my beloved father, and following the service, we all went by car to a nearby Jewish cemetery for his burial. My mother would be laid to rest next to him eleven years later. My Uncle Bernie and Aunt Harriet were also buried in the same cemetery a short distance away. They were all wonderful people in my life, and I still think about all of them almost every day.

In the summer of 2002, Jeri's mother, Ruth, telephoned Jeri to advise her she was again receiving ongoing treatment for her recurring bladder cancer that so far had been held well in check. By then, Ruth had already sold her lovely home in Lantana, FL, and moved to a very tasteful first-floor condo apartment in a large community in Lake Worth, FL, called "The Fountains." Jeri and I had visited Ruth on a few occasions when we went to Florida following our wedding. But the last time was the most difficult for us because Ruth's bladder cancer had by then spread, and she had been taken to Hospice care at the nearby JFK Medical Center. She received very excellent care from the attending nurses, who treated her with the most comforting end-of-life possible. Jeri and I, plus her brother Paul, were there to say our respective goodbyes to a truly gracious woman who herself had gone through hell with MS when she had been even younger than Jeri was when she was first diagnosed. After Ruth's death, we held a small commemorative service for her with only a few close friends. We miss her very much.

In 2003-2004, I remember having foot surgeries on both my feet, the first to correct the bunion on my left big toe and relax the hammertoes in my left foot. The very next year, I had corrective surgery on the bunion of my right big toe, as well as relaxing the hammertoes in my right foot. I mention these surgeries here because, by this time, I was no longer running or jogging in the streets, pounding the pavement as I had done for at least ten years. But my intention had always been to keep doing cardio at a local gym until they had to carry me away. My improved toes allowed me to continue using the various cardio machines that were then available, and I still use them today, twenty years later. I recommend to all to keep exercising as much as you can within the limits of your own body. If you need surgery, get it, and don't use that as an excuse for no longer exercising. Exercising has been a godsend for me because, without it, I might not have ended up healthy and strong enough to take care of myself and Jeri. I think of exercise as a pathway to a better life for your body and your mind.

One of the physical issues I have had to deal with over the past several years has been Gastroesophageal Reflux Disease, or GERD. I have basically kept it under control for many years with proper diet and prescription medications with proton pump inhibitors, which create a prolonged reduction of stomach acid that can cause increased reflux. For the past three-plus years, I have also eliminated coffee in the morning and substituted herbal teas instead. I find herbal teas to be quite pleasant and do not adversely affect me with reflux, heartburn, or spasms like coffee with caffeine had done to me. I have never eaten many fast foods or spicy foods for nutrition reasons, but I have also stayed away from them even more now than I did before. I believe in being proactive in using preventive medicine to avoid medical issues before they ever become major health problems, including getting regular colonoscopies and endoscopies, as recommended, on a regular basis and being screened by MRIs, CAT Scans, and other diagnostic medical devices to prevent illnesses and diseases before they become fatal.

This brings me to one of my major pet peeves in life: food manufacturers are killing Americans with too much sugar and sodium. There is simply no reason for it except the U.S. Food and Drug Administration (FDA) apparently either doesn't have the authority to tell the food manufacturers how much sugar and sodium it can put into our foods, or it doesn't really care how many Americans are dying from too much sugar and sodium in their diets. It's like the food manufacturers are given total freedom to pour in as many excessive amounts of sugar and sodium as they want. They would save money by not putting so much into our food. Why are they in everything to such excess, including breakfast cereals, muffins, desserts, ice cream, and so many other foods? I'm not suggesting there should not be any sugar and sodium added to food production, but why can't the amounts be significantly reduced to save lives? I have already gone on Twitter several times asking food manufacturers to please stop pouring all that s- - t into the foods we eat. We can add our own sugar and sodium to the taste we want. We don't need Big Brother doing it for us.

About five years into our marriage, suddenly, in 2003-04, Jeri had an unknown physical breakdown or abnormality. Suddenly, her legs didn't work well enough to keep her on her feet and walk like she had been able to before. I took her to a neurologist in Hartford who did some tests and opined that Jeri might be in the early stages of Multiple Sclerosis. Jeri's mother had had it, too, but was able to mostly overcome it in her later years. Following the initial diagnosis, an MRI was done on Jeri's spine, neck, and head. The doctor confirmed his initial opinion that Jeri had Multiple Sclerosis, a degenerative neurological disease. By then, Jeri had now become totally bedridden and couldn't go to work for at least a few months. She remained in bed in our upstairs bedroom during the entire ordeal. The doctor described this episode of being in bed for a long time as an exacerbation of the disease. The doctor authorized a visiting nurse to come to our condominium to complete a five-day intravenous infusion of high doses of Methylprednisolone (Solu-Medrol), which is a family of corticosteroids. The results were very encouraging, and Jeri was able to gradually start walking again with the help of a physical therapist.

She soon went back to work and began a regimen of a once-weekly steroid injection into the leg. The exacerbation was over, although there is never an end to Multiple Sclerosis in the life of someone who has it. For the next several years, Jeri was able to walk normally for her. But what was normal for Jeri would still be less than adequate for most people, just ambling along at a slow pace. However, we still had fun. In most of the following years, we were able to take vacations on several ocean cruises, and Jeri was, for the most part, fine. On one of the early cruises, we went to Turkey, Greece, and Israel.

On another cruise, we went from Rome to Barcelona. Still, another started in Stockholm, Sweden, then to Helsinki, Finland, Oslo, Norway, Tallinn, Estonia, and onto St. Petersburg, Russia. One of our cruises left from Copenhagen, Denmark, and stopped in Amsterdam, the Netherlands, Brussels, and Bruges, Belgium, along the way. We even took a guided group tour and visited Northern Italy, including Milan and Lake Como. We have also been on cruises that stopped in Florence and at least a few times in Venice. And we've also been on several cruises to the Caribbean and the West Indies.

In May 2009, I took Sasha out of her crate one day after work and began to take her for a walk when she suddenly stopped in the street, let out a hellacious roar, and fell over. At first, I wanted to believe she may have had just some sort of breathing problem. I didn't want to admit that what I just witnessed was a fatal heart attack. But it was. I took her lifeless body back to the condo, called the veterinarian, and drove there with our dead dog. The veterinarian confirmed to me that, indeed, she was dead. I called Jeri, still at work, to ask her if she wanted to say goodbye to Sasha, but she didn't want to do so. So dear Sasha was now just dust sitting in a little bin in my bathroom closet. She surely deserved better for her 11 years on earth. I have always regretted the circumstances surrounding our life with Sasha, but our work took priority over her. I told Jeri that if we ever got another dog, I wanted to give it much more of my personal time and love than Sasha had ever received.

We waited an entire year before we looked for another Shih-Tzu. In May 2010, we again saw an advertisement in the Hartford Courant for Shih-Tzu puppies, this time in New Britain. We drove over to the house and saw three adorable, two-month-old puppies frolicking, rolling over each other, and playing only as puppies can. We learned there had been a litter of four, but one puppy had already been taken. After watching the three of them go non-stop for an hour or so in the woman's living room, I looked at Jeri to see if she had any preference. She said it was up to me. I picked the biggest of the three because I liked her face more than the others. So off we went with the owner's dog named Lindsey, whom we renamed Marlee. She was big for a Shih-Tzu, weighing in at 18-19 lbs. as a mature dog. Again, because we were still working, Marlee had to be crated during the day. But it was only for one year because I retired on June 30, 2011, and Jeri retired from her position on August 1.

My retirement from DRS was long overdue. I had put in twenty years of hard work right up to my age of 69 1/2. I had thought about retiring earlier, but nothing came of my previous efforts to find a suitable job in Florida that paid nearly as much money. I never felt that I ever cheated the taxpayers of the State of Connecticut, who ultimately paid my salary and benefits, because I believed they deserved my very best efforts. Unfortunately, that mindset may not have been commonplace and shared by enough employees in the State workforce. I think too many, especially those in executive positions, may have regarded their positions as relatively cushy jobs in which they did not have to work too hard, and some of them were, in fact, obtained through political patronage. Mine was not. I believed in working hard for all concerned: the State, my fellow employees, and myself. When I retired, my colleagues in the law department and others in the agency held an informal noon retirement party for me, which Jeri was invited to and attended.

I then started the two-month process of packing up our clothing and other belongings into nearly thirty boxes and took many of our unneeded furnishings, other personal possessions, and even framed pieces of art to Goodwill. I went back and forth from our condo to Goodwill in Canton, CT, so many times the manager of the Goodwill store and I greeted each other on a first-name basis. I did not wish to ship all those things to our home in Florida because there simply was not enough room for all that we had both accumulated over many years. We hired a mover to transport the larger pieces of furniture we wanted to retain, plus the many boxes I had packed up. Our drive down from Connecticut with Marlee took us about two and a half days to our home in Port St. Lucie, FL. She was a great traveler. I would stop along the way to allow all of us time to pee. In north Florida, we came to a rest stop where a woman had a beautiful pet rabbit outside that was about the size of Marlee, and she took a liking to it. We had never seen one like that before or since. A few days after we finally arrived at our home, the modern furniture we had bought at a store in Massachusetts for our Florida home also arrived. Our new life was beginning to take shape.

When we first started looking for homes in Florida, we went to Palm Beach County but found that the prices of the homes and the property taxes were much higher than we had expected. The real estate agent was understanding, and, in fact, she was the one who suggested we should look at homes in our community in Port St. Lucie because she knew I was seeking a more contemporary home. The community itself is quite unique because of its large size, the fact it has manned security both in the front and back entries and the many different prices available in the various sub-associations within the community. In addition, just outside of the main entry gate, there is a complex of top semi-private golf courses with its own clubhouse and dining room. Many of the residents who live here are "snowbirds" who spend their winters in Florida but go north for the summers to get out of the heat.

Our home is not as big or expensive as many other homes in the community, but it's large enough and comfortable for the two of us. The home has 2,240 sf under air, all on one level, with ceilings as high as fifteen feet, three bedrooms, two baths, and a nice-sized screened lanai in the back of the house off the master bedroom and the kitchen. Our house has the biggest garage on the street, which is a feature that enables us to also have much-needed extra storage space that many homes lack. The house also has an open-landscape, contemporary design that is very appealing, although we wish we had another bedroom because one of the bedrooms we use as an office. When we arrived at the home, there were many things that needed attention, like most houses do. We especially needed a new HVAC system because the condenser outside and the main unit inside were quite old and very dirty. We have since replaced that HVAC system once again because, unfortunately, there are some air conditioning companies that just don't do the work very well here in Florida. In addition, nearly five years ago, we replaced the original concrete tile roof on our house, which was built in 1994.

Our house is one of eighteen on our street. For most of the twelve years we've lived here, our next-door neighbor to the right of us, facing the street, was a woman from Ireland named Cathy R., to whom both Jeri and I took an immediate liking. In fact, we both grew to love Cathy. She was undoubtedly one of the nicest, kindest women we have ever met. For several years after we first moved to Florida, Cathy would make Thanksgiving dinners for us and any of her family members who happened to come down to Florida to be with her. Cathy and her late husband, John, who unfortunately passed away about a year before we moved to Florida, had six daughters who grew up to be very successful in their work. We had met John on a few of our previous trips to Florida when we came here to hire some workers to paint the house and make renovations to our home prior to moving in. Cathy was a one-of-a-kind woman with a heart of gold who was beloved by all who knew her. She was also a terrific cook and baker and had a wonderful green thumb to be able to grow almost any flowering plant. About six years ago, Cathy was the Grand Marshal of the St. Patrick's Day Parade held here in Port St. Lucie.

Somehow, she managed to include Jeri and her sister-in-law, Chris, in the car with her for the short trip in and around the streets of our local Civic Center, waving to the crowd of people who gathered on both sides of the street to see her and those who marched behind, including me and a few of Cathy's daughters who flew down to see their mother for the occasion. I cannot say enough about what Cathy has meant to us during the many years she lived here. Unfortunately, she now has dementia and lives in a memory care nursing home in New York City. She was living with her daughter Maureen in her apartment in New York City until she started having falls that contributed further to her mental breakdown. It is very sad to see a woman like her end up like this after living such a full and devout Catholic life in which she used to go to church every morning.

A few days after we arrived in Florida and had unpacked most of the boxes, we went to the local Florida Motor Vehicles Department to get our new driver's licenses. All was going well for another week until reality set in that reminded us of Jeri's continuing problem trying to cope with her MS. That weekend, we decided to go to an Italian Fair next to a nearby shopping center, one exit down from where we live. At the time, Jeri had not yet been using a cane to get around. She was able to walk on her own but at a slower pace than most people. As we were walking from our car to the Italian Fair, we were about to enter a driveway from the street in front of the Fair when Jeri simply lost her balance and fell right on her face, knocking out teeth and incurring damage to her face, and especially over one eye, turning it bright red.

It was the first of many falls Jeri would have over the next twelve-plus years due to her Multiple Sclerosis. It took many weeks of healing for Jeri to get back to where she had been. That experience hastened our search for a neurologist who could help Jeri with her MS. Living in this gated community in Port St. Lucie has been a comfortable place to live, although we do not participate in most of the social activities available here. But there are simply not enough qualified doctors here, especially for people with diseases like MS. But we were able to find a doctor who had MS patients up in Palm Bay, FL, which is one hour north of us on I-95. He prescribed appropriate medicine for Jeri, but our appointments with him were long and tiring because the doctor always overbooked the number of patients for each half-hour in the mornings. For the most part, Jeri was able to keep her MS under control for several years after that with the guidance and supervision of that doctor and other neurologists. But frankly, there are not enough doctors familiar with treating MS patients.

Jeri and I lived about an hour and a half north of where my mother lived in Coconut Creek, FL, in Broward County. After we moved to Florida on or about September 21, 2011, we tried to spend as much of our time with her as possible despite the distance between us.

But in early January 2012, I called my mother, and she told me she was having a problem with her breathing. I offered to take her to her doctor there, but she said her neighbor could take her the short distance to get to the doctor just outside the main gate. I called her again later to find out if she had seen her doctor. She told me he had prescribed some pills for her that had given her "the runs." That was the last time I ever spoke to mother. Early the next morning, I received a telephone call from my Sister Janet telling me mom had passed away that night at 91.

I was so shocked. Jeri and I immediately drove to the hospital and went to the room in which my mother was lying. I also met with the hospital doctor to ask what had happened, and he opined that she must have had pneumonia, which led to a fatal heart attack. But we never learned what kind of pills my mother's local doctor had given her. I really do not trust doctors in Florida, now having lost both my parents to what may have been incorrect initial diagnoses. A few days later, my mother was buried next to my father after a small funeral.

In the latter part of 2015, Jeri's condition worsened significantly. Suddenly, she started falling in our bedroom and elsewhere in the house, especially in late November. It was at that same time Jeri received a panicked telephone call from the wife of Jeri's brother, Paul, who lived in

Phoenix, AZ, who himself had some of the same MS symptoms as Jeri but failed to seek medical help. Paul was a good man, then about age 64, but was a very different kind of person than Jeri in many ways.

In some earlier years before that, he had owned as many as six well-known motorcycles at the same time and maybe just as many kinds of guns and knives he kept in his bedroom. But he did not take care of himself well enough. He smoked cigarettes and pot and drank too much alcohol, all of which exacerbated an uncared-for, probable MS medical condition that Jeri believes did him in way before his time. The call Jeri received from Paul's wife on a Sunday evening advised her that Paul had gone to his refrigerator Thursday night, fell back, hit the back of his head on the floor, and never recovered consciousness. Note that Paul's wife never called Jeri until three days after Paul had already died. At that very moment, Jeri could not even walk with a cane because she had fractured both wrists in a fall at home just a few days before. Paul's wife implored Jeri to get out to Phoenix as soon as possible for his funeral. But Jeri was in absolutely no condition to travel. Paul's wife didn't understand Jeri's situation and never spoke to her again, thinking the worst of Jeri for not attending the funeral. We surely would have gone, if possible, but Jeri's MS had prevented it. Jeri's falls in that span of time included not only two broken wrists but also a few cracked ribs and another break in some capped teeth. Jeri's medicine was changed, and so was her doctor. Instead of heading one hour north to Palm Bay, we started seeing another neurologist in Palm Beach Gardens, FL, which is nearly one hour south of us. These are part of the ups and downs of MS, never really knowing when the condition will radically change for the worse. And never really had a good enough neurologist to take care of her.

In February 2015, I already had the first of my two back surgeries that required spinal fusion of the L4-L5 vertebrae. Since I had first arrived in Florida, I had been seeing doctors provide injections into my spinal column to ease the pinched nerve and the resulting sciatica pain behind my right knee. But, the injections did not eliminate the problem and only eased the pain for a given period. Following the surgery, I had physical therapy for several weeks and walked as much as I could in accordance with the surgeon's recommendations. I healed in about three months or so and started back to the gym. I was happy to be back working on the cardio and weight machines. I missed seeing some of the people I had met there. The back condition I had is not uncommon among many people in their 60s or 70s. But I believe mine was also exacerbated by many years of pounding the streets of Westport in the 1980s. I truly loved running for the euphoric feeling I got every morning, but I later paid a dear price with the sciatica pain and the back surgeries I had to correct the condition.

A year went by, and I began to again feel the sciatica pain behind my right knee. In July 2016, I had another more comprehensive back surgery that placed long rods in my back extending from L5 up to L2 with appropriate nuts and bolts. Knock on wood, my back has not given me any problems since. I have diligently gone to the gym to do back, chest, and arm exercises on the weight machines and continued doing different forms of cardio on treadmills, spin bikes, elliptical machines, rowing machines, and others. To be successful long-term, I think back surgeries do require patients to continue getting stronger and more muscular afterward, especially in the lower back, and to physically improve what the doctor did to help get my back to where it needed to be. I have nothing but praise for Dr. Daniel H., and I am grateful he was also able to help Jeri four years later. I hope he continues to help many hundreds more patients live more pain-free lives before he retires.

In the summer of 2019, I decided I needed a vacation for myself. I had never gone anywhere by myself for a long period of time. I had been very impressed with China during the previous one-week cruise Jeri, and I had taken from Hong Kong to Shanghai and Beijing four or five years before. I think Shanghai is the biggest of all the cities in China, followed by Beijing. I have seen a lot of traffic in New York City, but I thought Beijing may have had just as much or more. It also had an amazing underground mall under our hotel with stores selling only high-end women's clothing and jewelry. In early July 2019, I booked a solo vacation for me to South China for two weeks. With all the walking that would be involved, it would have been impossible for Jeri to walk so far there and keep up the pace needed for me to see the sights I wished to see. I first took a flight from West Palm Beach to JFK Airport. Sitting next to me on the flight was a friendly couple from Taiwan. The wife, Ivy W., and I talked during almost the entire trip. I'm not sure whether her husband did not know English as well as she did or was just more reticent than her. But she happens to be an English teacher for her students in a grade school in Taipei. I am still trying to stay in touch with Ivy W. on Facebook.

After I arrived at JFK, there was about a three-hour layover until my flight at 1:00 am to Guangzhou. It was the longest flight I had ever been on, and I was tired. Despite having paid much more for business class, I could not sleep on the airplane. Maybe I was just too anxious to get there. The airport in Guangzhou was seemingly quite new and very big. I got a taxi to my hotel and spent as much time as I could sleeping over the next several hours to catch up to my jet lag.

The time difference between Guangzhou and New York is 12 hours ahead. I only spent three days in that city, but they were quite memorable. Meals were available in the hotel on one of the top floors overlooking the city. The first thing I noticed up there was the unmistakable smog hovering over the city because it is an older industrial city that, for many years, likely did not have any air pollution restrictions. But it is nevertheless a city with much character. The next day, I was up, raring to go. Down the street from the hotel, I took a city bus with the locals to see some of the sights of the city. I had no idea where I was going, but with a little map, I could figure out some of the destinations.

The second day I was there, I walked quite a bit around the streets surrounding the perimeter of the hotel. I even bought a tee shirt and shorts because my luggage had been held up somewhere at the airport. But I finally got it the second night. On the third day, I was fortunate to have obtained a rather rare one-to-one tour of the city with a nice young man who took me to see many good sights in that city, including Shamian Island overlooking a river, where people congregate on Saturday mornings to talk, do group exercise and play cards. I also went to the

Chen Clan Ancestral Hall, which has many beautiful Chinese artifacts and an actual Buddhist Temple and then had lunch at a well-attended local Chinese restaurant.

That afternoon, I had a driver take me from the hotel in Guangzhou to my next hotel in Shenzhen, a few hours away, for the balance of the trip. My hotel there was well-located next to and over a subway stop, with nearby outdoor food cafeterias, sit-down restaurants, and fruit stands. This is a much newer city than Guangzhou, just north of Hong Kong, with many subway stops, each of which seemed like their own separate city. I enjoyed riding the subways with the Chinese because they are good, pleasant people, not at all troublesome or bothersome like some who ride the New York City subways, for example. In fact, the Chinese very much respect their elders, and some young women even offered me their seats when I was standing. I think Americans should take note of the positive way Chinese grandparents take care of their grandchildren so their children can go to work. This is how they conduct day-care. I enjoyed my time in Shenzhen very much. I also rode in taxis there, which in 2019 were already all-electric vehicles.

For those in the USA who still think the Chinese ride around in rickshaws, think again. There are likely more high-end expensive cars in China than in our country or anywhere else in the world. There are many, many thousands of them in the big cities throughout China. Each day, I set off for a new destination on the subway. One of my favorite stops was going to Lianhuashan Park on Saturday morning to see the people dance with each other under a big tree. It is a big park for walking around in open space with many trails and trees throughout. Another of my favorite stops was the section of the city where artists still thrive. It was raining for part of that morning, but I could not leave there without buying a piece of original artwork from one of the master painters. And I took it by hand from Shenzhen on two flights all the way back to my home in Port St. Lucie, FL. I show it with pride on a wall in my living room. I still have not seen Hong Kong to the same extent as I've seen Shenzhen, but I hope to do so in the future.

You know, as I do that 2020 was not a good year for most people in the world. And it was even worse for us. We didn't know COVID would be a problem for us until about the middle of March. But by then, we had already scheduled Jeri for lumbar surgery on March 17, 2020, to correct her spine that was forcing her to walk bent over like an old hag, but she was only 72 at the time. Jeri had her surgery on that date and recovered relatively well with physical therapy into late April. The surgeon also recommended that Jeri have the additional surgery she needed to correct the Scoliosis in her upper back. The only question was how soon after the previous surgery she would have the Scoliosis surgery. The surgeon favored sooner rather than later. I thought maybe the fact Jeri has progressive MS would weigh in favor of having the surgery later in June, but the surgeon, who was obviously not very busy during the pandemic, favored having the surgery in May. And May 20, 2020, was the date of Jeri's second surgery for correction of her Scoliosis.

Like the first surgery, Jeri came through this surgery well. But she had now been on heavy doses of Oxycodone for pain for over two months, and her balance was especially not good, given her usual balance challenges with MS, plus the effects of the pain medicine. One night in May, about a week after her surgery, Jeri fell in the bathroom on her back and felt something give in her lower back. We made an appointment to visit the surgeon, who confirmed that Jeri had indeed displaced the rod in her lower back that was inserted to correct her L4-L5 issue. So, another surgery needed to be scheduled. My recollection is that Jeri's third surgery was on June 12, 2020. However, this time, having had three surgeries so close in time, Jeri suffered a major exacerbation of her MS, which left her immobile in bed unable to walk for about one year.

Following her hospital stay for the third surgery, Jeri was sent to a nearby rehabilitation hospital for nearly a month. Without me being consulted, Jeri was then sent to a local nursing home for about four days. I was concerned she had not been receiving her MS infusion medicine for a long time, so I sought her discharge from the nursing home to take her for her MS treatment medicine and then took her home. It was then the last week in July 2020. But I needed nursing care for Jeri because she was bedridden. I didn't really know any visiting nurses in Florida. However, we used the Visiting Nurse Association of Connecticut when Jeri needed her infusion of Solu-Medrol way back in 2004.

So, I called the Visiting Nurse Association of Florida. They sent out a few "nurses" two times per week to care for the heels of Jeri's feet, which had become very sore, lying in beds for so long. They did help to heal Jeri's heels, but they also did nothing to stop the growth and festering of three deep ulcerated bed sores on Jeri's left backside without ever telling us to use an air mattress on her bed until they had already seen Jeri for nearly a month. I had never seen bedsores, but they resemble tunnels into the body that keep growing wider and deeper without stopping unless suitable wound care is applied. After the bed sores had already gotten out of control, the "nurses" then decided to request two wound care specialists from their company to be assigned to Jeri's case.

For more than three weeks, they diligently tried to stop the wounds from getting worse but finally gave up and requested that Jeri be sent to the local hospital here in Port St. Lucie to prevent further damage to her body. Jeri was at the hospital receiving wound care for three weeks and five days when, unbeknownst to me and without our consent, she was sent to one of the most depressing nursing homes I have ever seen, located in Royal Palm Beach, FL. While it did provide continuing wound care for Jeri, sending in a doctor once a week to clean and tend to her bedsores, like most of its services, there were simply not enough staff members to pay attention to Jeri's other needs, including providing physical therapy to address her MS exacerbation to allow her to get out of bed and get some exercise.

Jeri was there for nearly six months, from September 2020 to March 2021. However, the nursing home got even worse at the end of 2020 when it was sold to a different owner-operator who apparently let go of as many staff as it could in order to save money. The State of Florida seems not to care much, if at all, about the thousands of sick and elderly people who languish in their nursing homes without sufficient staff to take adequate care of them. It is a terrible situation that also likely exists in many other States, and I would like to see our federal government do something about remedying this awful situation. I don't expect anything from most do-nothing Republican politicians who seem to want to tear down our federal government. So, I am now speaking to leading Democrats in our country. If the USA is to truly provide proper care to those in need of nursing home services, we simply must do a much better job as a nation. Otherwise, the nursing homes should be closed by the Department of Health and Human Services (HHS), as administrator of both the Medicare and Medicaid programs in our federal government, for their extreme inadequacies and be replaced by an alternate form of more comprehensive nursing facilities that offer physical therapy and much better staffing of nurses, rather than be filled with mainly low-paid health aides who lack the training and discipline to provide the kind of good nursing care needed.

I made the one-hour trip south once every week to visit Jeri with our dog Marlee at the nursing home in Royal Palm Beach for the entire time she was there, from September 2020 to March 2021. Jeri's bedsores were tended to, but she never had what one would call physical therapy because the nursing home had no real physical therapists.

Some aides would occasionally come by from time to time to try to pick up Jeri's legs and move them somewhat, but it wasn't what one would call physical therapy. Jeri was still totally bedridden for nearly one year. I continually tried to get assistance from our medical insurance carrier, United Healthcare, but the staff I called didn't really help much at all. And I was never able to talk to any of their many top-echelon executives during that period. United Healthcare allegedly has over 300,000 US employees. However, I only managed to speak to a few of the lower-echelon employees who answered the company's telephone number. I had to go it alone. Finally, after six months of personal torment searching for help for Jeri online, I found a rehabilitation hospital called Neulife Rehabilitation Hospital in Mount Dora, FL, which is a self-pay facility for people with brain injuries. It agreed to pick up Jeri at the nursing home in Royal Palm Beach, FL, in the middle of March and transport her to its facility north of Orlando, FL, a ride of almost two and one-half hours.

Again, as with the previous nursing home Jeri was in, I would drive the one and a half hours each way with Marlee once each week for more than twenty weeks. I met some of the many patients there who knew Jeri, and I also became fond of the staff there. With the daily assistance of the facility's good physical therapy department, Jeri went from being totally bedridden to walking out of there with a rolling walker, called a rollator, on September 30, 2021, and with all the staff at the facility clapping their hands with pride for Jeri and for themselves doing a job well done. It was quite expensive, but well worth it. How can anyone put a value on what walking again is worth to someone who hasn't had the use of her legs for a year and might not have had it for the rest of her life if not for the fact we had enough money to pay such a good facility to rehabilitate her.

The experience we went through certainly suggests there must be many thousands of Americans in nursing homes each year who do not get that same chance at recovery to walk again simply because they lack the funds to obtain the same good quality physical therapy. And that's a darn shame because most of them pay federal taxes to help fund our federal government each year. However, the United States Department of Health and Human Services doesn't do nearly enough to give back their tax dollars and even try to help those same Americans get out of their wheelchairs and walk again.

I was pleased to take Jeri home again for nearly the first time in a year. Her bed sores had been healed, and she was now able to walk with the aid of a rollator. Almost two months passed before Jeri had another mishap. In

November, right around Thanksgiving, Jeri was at the edge of her bathroom and reached for a bathrobe in her hall clothes closet, and she fell. She broke the femur in her right leg. She needed another surgery, this time to put a rod in her leg to stabilize the femur during the healing process. She was now once again off her legs for the most part until late January or early February 2022. She recovered and then once again restarted her physical therapy to help her walk with a rollator. Jeri was fine for another year. But in early March of 2023, Jeri once again reached for something, this time a calendar on the wall in the kitchen. And once again, she fell on her backside, opening one of the bedsores from two to three years ago.

Since March, Jeri has had home health visits a few times each week from a nursing service to clean and disinfect the bedsores. I also took Jeri to a wound center at the local hospital here a few times per month for two or three months, and I have been doing the wound cleansing and disinfection myself almost every day for several months right up to the present. The wound center was not pleased with the progress, so we were sent to another wound care specialist who works in a doctor's office. The woman there had some other ideas on how to treat the bedsore. But after several months under her care, Jeri's wound does not appear to be closer to being healed.

It seems like each of the wound care specialists attempted their own method to heal bedsores, from using a portable wound vacuum that sucks out the impurities and dries it up a bit to inserting a variety of different biologicals inside the wound to get it to close. Frankly, I was tired of doing this wound care for Jeri for more than six months and being sent from one wound care center to another. I also became worn out being Jeri's caregiver in general because, at times, I just felt like a slave rather than her husband. I would much prefer to spend my free time enjoying life rather than continuing to do what I have been doing for Jeri for most of the last four years. But duty calls.

Jeri has always been a truly kind, good-natured woman who likely has most of the virtues I spoke about in my Preface. On and after 2020, when the stock markets first came tumbling down due to COVID, and then a few years later because of the Russian invasion of Ukraine, our stocks have taken a beating in value to an extent I've never seen in all the years I've been an investor. Throughout our marriage, I paid most of our living expenses, including our mortgage, property taxes and insurance, electric and water bills, food, vitamin supplements, and most restaurant bills. Jeri has always paid the quarterly estimated taxes to the IRS and occasionally pays for food. We each had our own checking and savings accounts, and it has always worked out well for us to have this division of our finances.

My overall experiences on the Internet have been mostly very good. On Facebook, I have made many new friendships and rekindled friendships with both men and women who I first met when we were young adults or even children. For example, I go a long way back with some people from my childhood, like Tommy S., Norm A., Jimmy W., Michael F., Stan W., Steve S., Willie D., Jonathan F., Remy Z., Beth M., Judith S., Roberta L., Jane F-L, Gail W., Laurence L., Louise S., Marvin L., Joe W. I hope to remain in contact with these and other people I've known since I was an older teenager, like William W., Camilo M., Jim Mc., Peter W., Daniel T., Richard E., Susan S., Susan L R., Arthur F., Ann S-Y, Susann P H., Ruth H., Robert L., Elaine C L., Gail L., Edward P., because we've shared friendships dating back to our earlier days.

In our lives, there always seem to be some unfortunate issues to deal with. In January 2023, our beautiful dog, Marlee, who would have been 13 in March, began to show signs of severe discomfort on her walks with me. She had never shown any real health problems before this. But now, she suddenly was stopping to pee many, many times along our walks. At first, I thought maybe it was just a temporary issue, but it persisted for a few more weeks. And then, I took her to a veterinarian facility in Port St. Lucie.

I frankly thought the attending veterinarian that day was somewhat disappointing in failing to spend more time with Marlee and attempt to test her more thoroughly. At certain times during this more than two-week period, Marlee had been exhibiting a great deal of pain, vigorously shaking her entire body while seated in her bed in the kitchen.

The next day, I made an appointment with another local veterinarian in St. Lucie West, who we used to go to when we first arrived here in September 2011. His staff tested Marlee with greater care and found that not only did she have a blockage in her bladder, but she also had tumors in one lung that were likely cancerous. We had been prepared to pay for surgery that day to relieve the blockage in Marlee's bladder. But once it became clear from x-rays taken earlier in the day that she had this other more fatal issue, the veterinarian recommended that she be put to sleep. As we said our final goodbyes to this wonderful, sweet dog, I broke down in front of Jeri and Marlee and cried like I had never cried as an adult.

Marlee was such a good companion for over twelve years, with a heart and soul that I never thought possible in any animal. She was the sweetest dog we ever knew. Although never overly affectionate, she would give us kisses upon request. I thought we would have a few more years with Marlee, but that was just not to be the case.

In August 2023, I received a letter from the office of my long-time urologist, Dr. David F., advising that he had suddenly passed away.

It was a big surprise to me because he was the most caring and compassionate physician I ever knew, and he was still working in his middle-to-late 70s right up until his death because he wanted to continue serving his patients until his end. He was such a good human being.

Our marriage was very challenging, principally due to the continuing physical challenges Jeri had faced since her first MS diagnosis in 2004. I had given Jeri a lot of love and personal sacrifice over our previous twenty-five years of marriage just trying to make her life more comfortable after she had fallen so many times, breaking so many bones in her body, and been in such serious difficulties arising from her long-term battle with MS. As such, I had much greater responsibilities than most husbands do, trying to pick her up off the floor so many times. And every time she fell, a piece of me went down, too.

For the previous twelve years, I had done almost everything: the grocery shopping, meal preparation, cooking and cleanup, doing the laundry every week, cleaning the house when our cleaning lady could not make it here, taking Jeri to her MS infusions for many years, and later her chemotherapy, and to her many other doctors' appointments with her primary care physician, her various neurologists, her rheumatologist, her gastroenterologist, and to her many MRI and CAT scan tests, and blood drawings. I also maintained the areas around the outside of our house with new flowering plants, little palm trees, and bougainvillea bushes that provided some beautification to the outside areas.

When we first moved to Florida, Jeri had bought some Phalaenopsis orchid plants. She knew I loved flowers and pretty plants, so I'd also keep taking care of them too. I really hadn't received from Jeri much of the love and affection I would have desired from my wife. But I also fully realized Jeri was just not often able to feel romantic living with the pain, suffering, and very unfortunate circumstances she lived with. But I always knew Jeri had an abiding respect for me, trust in me, and genuine love for me.

In early August 2023, out of nowhere, Jeri, who had just turned 75, began to have fluid form in her stomach that was so noticeable it made her look like she was having a baby, perhaps in her third term. I took her to a local medical facility near us, now owned by Cleveland Clinic here in Port St. Lucie, FL. It did a series of tests and then authorized Jeri to go to its affiliated hospital, located in the Tradition area, the next day for further examination. In my opinion, the state of medicine in 2023 is not very good because even people with good health insurance cannot, on short notice, obtain needed appointments with appropriate medical specialists in most cases. So, patients must instead go to the emergency rooms in their local hospitals for treatment. There are simply not enough medical specialists here in Port St. Lucie to be able to handle the ever-increasing numbers of people moving here.

At 6:30 a.m. the next morning, Jeri and I went to the emergency room at that hospital. Jeri was then formally admitted to the hospital and remained there for six days, undergoing more tests. Her stomach and lungs were both drained of the fluid. The test results found cancer cells in the fluid forming in her stomach as well as in her left lung.

I then made an appointment with a gynecological cancer doctor in a medical group in Orlando, FL. We were able to get an early appointment with the doctor, who just happened to know the doctor at the medical facility in

Port St. Lucie, where Jeri had been receiving the infusions of her MS medicine for several years.

We drove an hour and a half north to the medical complex adjacent to the hospital there, met with the doctor, and examined Jeri. He recommended Jeri start a regimen of chemotherapy for eight weeks. He never told us that Jeri's symptoms were basically fatal. However, Jeri received her eight chemotherapy infusions, and I began to maintain and even help to increase her weight during this period by cooking as much appetizing food as I could make her. And all the while, she lost all of her hair due to the chemotherapy.

Jeri was then fighting a three-way battle against what was believed to be ovarian cancer; at the same time, she was still being treated for her reopened bed sores from four years ago, as well as always being challenged by her continuing MS affliction. She was always such a brave woman who never gave up on overcoming what came her way. And she knew I was there by her side, trying to do the best I could to help her get through the troubled periods. Perhaps if we had been told the truth about Jeri's cancer, I could have taken her on a wonderful cruise around the world rather than having her suffer two months of deadly chemotherapy that did nothing but possibly just delay the inevitable for a few months.

Following the two months of chemotherapy, Jeri gradually seemed to be getting much better for several more months. Her hair grew back, and she seemed stronger and more capable of walking with the walker and exercising. We brought in health aides daily to help Jeri with her physical rehabilitation, always thinking positively that she would get better. The first ones who came in were quite efficient in providing Jeri with the assistance she needed. In fact, the larger of the two women was also a very good cook who made several delicious dishes for Jeri and me. However, there was a bit of a personality clash between us, based on her own insecurity that I was somehow disrespecting her when I asked her not to make excessive comments to the nurses who visited us at home. Plus, she was very loud, and her bellowing voice could be heard throughout the house every day.

After a few months, I asked both not to return, and I hired two Haitian sisters who seemed to fit our personalities much better. Jeri and I became very close to them, and we treated them as part of our family since we were both quite pleased with their services.

They were with us beginning in early March 2024. A month or two later, Jeri was admitted to the local hospital for what appeared to be a routine Urinary Tract Infection caused by wearing a catheter for over six months because it would not cause Jeri's bedsores to be infected. She was then released to a Hospice company to help us with Jeri's medicines and its nursing services. The intervention of the Hospice company was understandable, given Jeri had been diagnosed with cancer several months before. But we never thought she would not survive because we were unfortunately led to believe that Jeri's two months of intensive chemotherapy would kill the cancer. However, from the time Jeri left the hospital, she became bedridden at home for the rest of her life, with no more walking and rehabilitation.

Beginning in the middle of May 2024, it became obvious to me that Jeri had started to decline. She began to sleep more and more. So, I asked a good friend of mine named Mark to come over to our house to meet Jeri. I told Jeri I had met Mark and a few others at the gym and that I wanted her to meet him, too. The two of them had a very good conversation for about half an hour, which pleased all of us. Soon after, Jeri needed more round-the-clock nursing services from the Hospice company.

On Saturday morning, June 1, I sat with Jeri in her bed at home, telling her how much I loved her and letting her know that it was okay for her to leave me so she didn't have to suffer anymore. As I spoke to her in her stupor, she was intently staring at me and apparently listening to everything I said in the presence of the male Hospice nurse and one of our health aides. All of a sudden, around 12:30 pm, the nurse noted Jeri had stopped breathing, and I had finally lost her. I then spent more than a few days crying off and on. Even now, just recalling those last moments with Jeri brings tears to my eyes.

As I previously stated, it would have been more helpful for us if the doctors had been honest and truthful about Jeri's conditions in early August 2023 rather than put her through so much additional pain and suffering, asking her to submit to the two months of chemotherapy. Given Jeri had suffered for so many years in her life with MS, why couldn't her doctors have been more honest about the prognosis of her metastatic Ovarian Cancer? I have lost a lot of respect for the entire big pharmaceutical industry and medical communities that keep seeking and receiving more financial benefits in prescribing chemotherapy for cancer victims with conditions like Jeri had instead of just telling us the truth and letting us make our own final decisions.

Our personal experience with cancer may well be similar to the experiences others have had. In hindsight, from the first time we met with the gynecological oncologist in Orlando, FL, we felt like maybe we were never really given an honest prognosis of Jeri's medical conditions. Instead of being really honest and transparent in their diagnosis, the doctors failed to be truthful that the chemotherapy would likely be nothing but a delaying tactic and that she very well might die anyway, so the chemotherapy would not really make any difference in Jeri's ability to survive. Frankly, I think chemotherapy is mostly a hoax on the American people because it does more to feather the nest of big business and all medical professionals involved rather than actually helping most serious cancer patients survive. Why is our country still without cures for most cancers? Is it because the pharmaceutical industry and medical professionals are still making too much money off of cancer? I would like to think my dear wife did not die as a result of corruption in our entire medical system.

Jeri and I had both decided a long time ago to be cremated rather than undergo gut-wrenching funerals without many people attending because neither of us had any family left, with the exception of children and grandchildren in New York State and my two sisters.

Nevertheless, I decided to assemble a relatively small gathering at our home to honor and celebrate Jeri's life with some kind of nonsectarian memorial service. For this purpose, I asked the chaplain in the Hospice company in Port St. Lucie to be the lead in such service, and I promised to donate money to him or the Hospice company. He agreed to do it when he visited me at home in early June to go over some of the arrangements for the memorial service at about the same time as Jeri was cremated.

Given that my daughter Geri had offered to help me with removing Jeri's personal effects when her school year in Monroe, NY, ended at the end of June, I thought that would be an appropriate time to hold the memorial service on Sunday, June 30. And I also invited the Hospice doctor and three nurses who cared for Jeri in the last month of her life. During the two weeks leading up to June 30, I must have called the Hospice chaplain at least two or three times just to make sure he was coming. But he never returned any of my calls and he failed even to text me.

So at 1:00 pm on June 30, when all of the seventeen family and friends had already gathered in our home, the Hospice chaplain was nowhere to be found. In addition, none of the other invitees from the Hospice company staff either came, texted, or called me, advising that they would not attend. So I decided to go ahead and speak to those assembled, most of whom had known or met Jeri, to talk about the sweet, good-natured woman she was and how much I would miss her. I don't remember what I said or how long I spoke, but I didn't put anyone to sleep.

For this service, I had set up an enlarged photo of Jeri on top of a large round glass coffee table in our living room, surrounded by smaller photos of her as a child and photos of both of us throughout our marriage. And in the center of all the photos was the pretty flowered Cloisonné urn that contained her ashes. It gave me great satisfaction to do this for Jeri because she would likely have rejected the idea as unnecessary. But it gave me some degree of closure to a marriage that was filled with a great deal of love between us to balance out the many years of Jeri's pain and suffering with MS.

Epilogue

I sincerely wish our federal government would make the greater funding of medical research a major priority to fast-track finding cures for so many neurological diseases, like dementia and Alzheimer's disease, Multiple Sclerosis, ALS, Parkinson's Disease, Muscular Dystrophy, Brain Tumors, Strokes, etc., and also so many different Cancers, instead of just hoping for some long overdue cures by so many different privately funded medical research teams of charitable organizations that have never accomplished much of anything in my opinion.

My brother-in-law Dennis D., the second husband of my former wife, Richard B., Jeri's father, Richard F., as well as actor Patrick S. and so many others who have died from pancreatic cancer perhaps could have been saved if our nation, as a world leader, had made more of a genuine commitment years ago to increase the funding of medical research and do much more to improve the lives of Americans stricken with such diseases than be beset by political in-fighting and even chicanery by do-nothing, misguided politicians who fail to provide the right kind of leadership to prevent such needless deaths. Instead, so many of those same politicians have sought to enact more and more tax cuts for their wealthy donors, impose severe abortion restrictions on women, or wish to shut down our government to cut spending. But more men and women are needed in positions of power in our country who will actively seek to accomplish beneficial, life-saving goals on behalf of those who elect them, including providing the needed funding for medical research to start finding cures for so many neurological diseases. Relying merely on private medical research funded by individual charitable organizations does not seem to be working enough.

Too many families must watch their loved ones suffer from the many neurological diseases that exist or say their goodbyes to those who die way before their time because there isn't nearly enough medical research being conducted by the federal government to do the work necessary to find cures for so many neurological diseases. For those who wish to work purely in a research lab don't need an MD or DO, but they do need a PhD or even a Masters' degree with significant experience.

The National Institutes of Health (NIH) is the primary agency of the US government responsible for biomedical and public health research. Many NIH facilities are in Bethesda, MD, and other nearby suburbs of the Washington D.C. metropolitan area, with other primary facilities in the Research Triangle in North Carolina and smaller satellite facilities located around the US. The NIH conducts its own scientific research through the NIH Intramural Research Program (IRP) and provides major biomedical research funding to non-NIH research facilities through its Extramural Research Program (ERP).

I have concluded from the information available on the Internet that most of the NIH research done for the past 30 years appears to have focused mainly on the Human Genome Project (HGP), which was an international scientific research project with the goal of determining the base pairs that make up human DNA, and of identifying, mapping and sequencing all of the genes of the human genome from both a physical and functional standpoint. However, based on the rather limited government medical research information being reported online, I cannot even conclude that the HGP was intended to provide a causal connection to finding a cure for most human neurological diseases.

Recently, the NIH seems to have begun issuing public relations research blogs through its IRP, one on August 15, 2023, and another on September 12, 2023, which seems to suggest our nation is still not very close to finding cures for the many neurological diseases. The earlier one, with the heading "IRP Discoveries Could Enhance Recovery from Brain Injuries," stated, "IRP scientists recently discovered how a particular type of cell in the blood stimulates the brain's construction crew to leap into action, potentially opening the door to treatments that boost healing in the brain." The latter one was entitled "Mouse Study Could Lead to New Therapies for a Variety of Ailments."

In it, the conclusion was: "In most parts of your brain, the set of neurons you're born with is what you've got for the rest of your life–just like your fingers and toes, if you lose any, they're not coming back. The body does have ways to encourage healing after a brain injury, but they are extremely constrained. However, by lending those natural systems a helping hand, IRP researchers have managed to dramatically boost the regeneration and recovery of vision in mice with damage to the nerves that connect the eyes to the brain, an approach that could one day help people recover from other types of nervous system injuries as well."

So, while it appears there currently is some advanced medical research being done now by the federal government's NIH into at least one form of regeneration and recovery from brain damage and a treatment that boosts healing in the brain, the IRP research still does not appear to have advanced nearly enough to be able to find cures for most human neurological diseases. Therefore, it appears our nation is just not doing enough to address this issue.

Many more qualified, specialized medical research clinicians are needed to do the research necessary to find cures to so many neurological diseases that really should have been attempted to be discovered many years ago. And that will require a lot of money to be added to our federal budget or reallocated from other budgeted resources for such purposes. I also believe our federal government should provide financial incentives for more doctors to go into medical research, perhaps at least for a minimum tour of duty to pay back their medical school expenses, as opposed to going directly into private medical practice, and should actively seek the recruitment of medical research clinicians to significantly increase the numbers involved in this research effort.

What better way to run a government is there than to spend an increased percentage of our federal budget on trying to find cures for neurological diseases to prevent so many Americans from suffering from them and being a drain on their families and our society at large?

I believe it is truly about time for the President and

Congress to spend more money on targeted medical research on neurological diseases and cancers. But it cannot happen unless there is a genuine commitment by the leaders in our country from both political parties to seek to find cures for so many diseases of the central nervous system. And like most other issues of national importance, I believe this one will require a groundswell of sociopolitical activism by Americans exhorting our political leaders to spend a greater percentage of our federal taxes on finding cures for so many neurological diseases rather than passively sit by allowing so many of our tax dollars perhaps to be wasted, for example, on continuing to fund a terribly overblown Pentagon national defense budget.

Perhaps the top mega billionaires in our country, like Jeff Bezos, Elon Musk, Bill Gates, Warren Buffett, Oprah Winfrey, and others, could greatly help the medical research effort to find cures for so many neurological diseases rather than seek to take well-to-do Americans on joyrides into outer space, or instead put their money into other rather limited, self-serving causes that don't help our country at all.

Frankly, I don't really know what these rich people or other rich people do with their money. But I would surely appreciate as many wealthy people as possible being involved in funding this medical research effort by the United States government to find cures for the many neurological diseases that Americans keep suffering from and the cancers they keep dying from.

It is long, long overdue, don't you think?

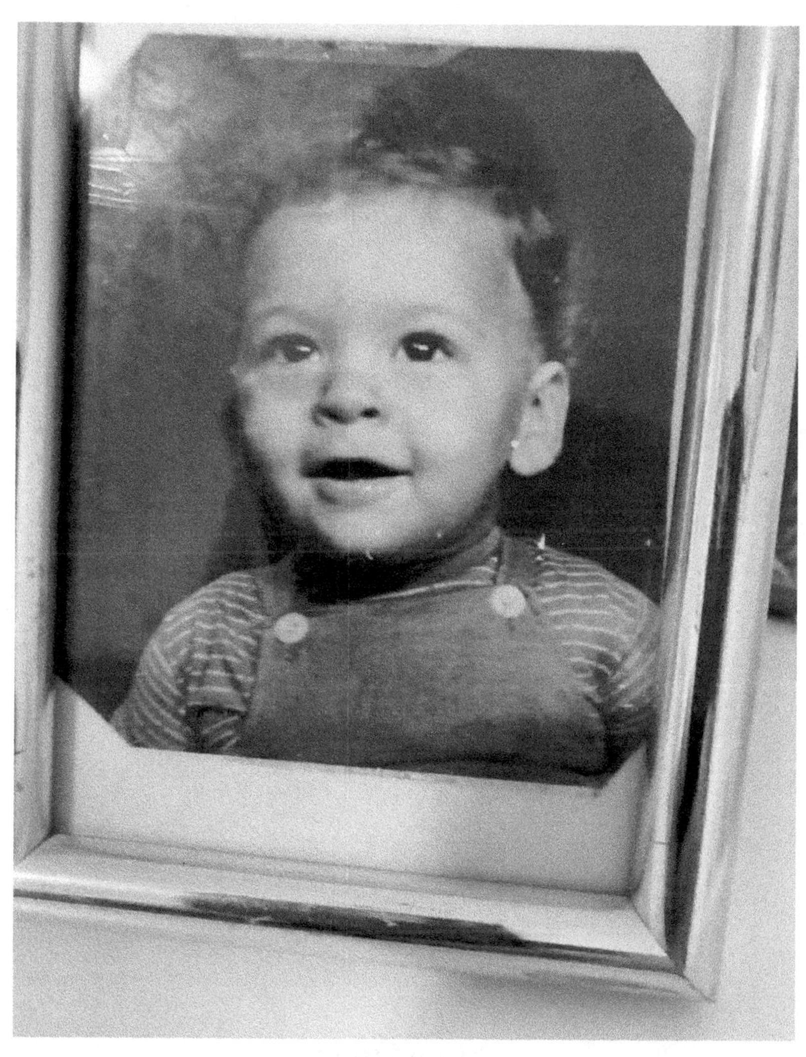

Baby Stuart

Little Stuart

Stuart And Father

Our Family At My Bar Mitzvah

Bar Mitzvah Boy

Hopkins Football Team (Number 2)

Eighth Grade Class (2nd Row, Fifth From Right)

14 Year Old Stuart At Hotel Pool

Stuart High School Graduation

My Granddad Benjamin

My Grandmother Sarah

My Grandmother Gussie

My Granddad Samuel (Front-Left)

Miss Irva Stahl

Miss Irva Stahl, Stuart Gollinger Will Wed In July

Mr. and Mrs. Jack Stahl of [illegible] Cromwell Road, Monroe, N.Y., announce the engagement of their daughter, Irva Russell, to Mr. Stuart Howard Gollinger, son of Mr. and Mrs. David Gollinger of [illegible] Chapel St.

Miss Stahl is a junior at Boston University, majoring in elementary education.

Mr. Gollinger prepared at Hopkins Grammar School, was graduated from Colby College in Waterville, Maine in [illegible] and will graduate from Suffolk Law School in Boston, Mass., this June.

A July wedding is planned.

Former Wife, Irva

Stuart With Beard (1980) And Owner Of Camera Shop In Westport Ct

Stuart Running 10k In Stamford, 1981

Mother And Father

Uncle Brud

Aunt Irene

Jeri And Stuart's Wedding Ceremony

Stuart And Jeri At The Wedding Reception

Marlee

Uncle Bernie And My Father

Jeri's Mother Ruth

Aunt Harriet And Uncle Bernie

Sister Janet And Dennis D.

My Daughter

1600 Chapel Street, New Haven, Ct

My Son's Family

My Daughter's Family

Stuart And Jeri

www.ingramcontent.com/pod-product-compliance
Lightning Source LLC
LaVergne TN
LVHW010547160826
845677LV00013B/3032

9798330511297